Physical Characteristics of the Golden Retriever

(from the Kennel Club's breed standard)

Colour

Any shade of gold or cream, neither red nor mahogany. A few white hairs, on chest only, permissible.

Coat

Flat or wavy with good feathering, dense water resisting undercoat.

Size

Height at withers: dogs 56–61 cms (22–24 ins); bitches 51–56 cms (20–22 ins).

Hindquarters

Loin and legs strong and muscular, good second thighs, well bent stifles (knees). Hocks (lower legs above the foot) well let down, straight when viewed from the rear, neither turning in nor out. Cow hocks (rear legs bending inward toward each other) highly undesirable.

Tail

Set on and carried level with the back, reaching to hocks, without curl at top.

Feet

Round and cat-like.

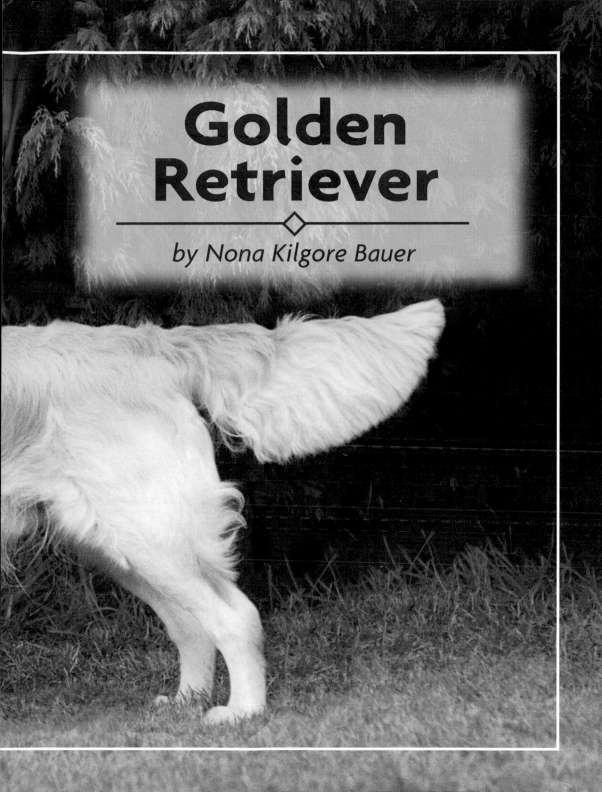

Golden Retriever

by Nona Kilgore Bauer

Table of Contents

9

19

DISTRIBUTED BY:

INTERPET
PUBLISHING

Vincent Lane, Dorking, Surrey RH4 3YX England

All rights reserved. No part of this book may be reproduced in any form, by photostat, scanner, microfilm, xerography or any other means, or incorporated into any information retrieval system, electronic or mechanical, without the written permission of the copyright owner.

ISBN 13: 978-1-902389-11-0

Copyright © 1999, **2007**
Kennel Club Books® A Division of BowTie, Inc.
Cover Design Patent: US 6,435,559 B2 • Printed in South Korea

79

Housebreaking and Training Your Golden Retriever

by Charlotte Schwartz
Be informed about the importance of training your Golden Retriever, from the basics of housebreaking, and understanding the development of a young dog, to executing obedience commands (sit, stay, down, etc.).

Photo Credits:
Norvia Behling
Carolina Biological Supply
Liza Clancy
David Dalton
Kent and Donna Dannen
Doskocil
Isabelle Francais
Gold-Rush Kennels
James Hayden-Yoav
James R. Hayden, RBP
Carol Ann Johnson
Dwight R. Kuhn
Dr. Dennis Kunkel
Alice Pantfoeder
Mikki Pet Products
Antonio Philippe
Phototake
Jean Claude Revy
Nikki Sussman
Karen Taylor
Alice van Kempen
C. James Webb
Thanks to
The Seeing Eye®
Morristown, NJ USA

Illustrations by Renée Low

136

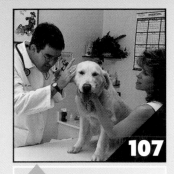

107

Health Care of Your Golden Retriever

Discover how to select a proper veterinary surgeon and care for your dog at all stages of life. Topics include vaccination scheduling, skin problems, dealing with external and internal parasites and the medical conditions common to the breed.

144

Your Senior Golden Retriever

Recognise the signs of an ageing dog, both behavioural and medical; Implement a senior-care programme with your veterinary surgeon and become comfortable with making the final decisions and arrangements for your senior Golden Retriever.

162

Understanding the Behaviour of Your Golden Retriever

Learn to recognise and handle common behavioural problems in your Golden Retriever, including aggression with people and other dogs, chewing, barking, mounting, digging, etc.

Showing Your Golden Retriever

Experience the dog show world, including different types of shows and the making up of a champion. Go beyond the conformation ring to working trials, field and agility trials, etc.

The Golden Retriever is the most beautiful and talented of the retriever breeds. It was originally developed to retrieve birds shot down over water. Dogs are trained, as shown here, with a dummy.

HISTORY OF THE
Golden Retriever

The youngest and most beautiful of the retriever breeds, the Golden Retriever was originally developed as a waterfowl dog. Although still an admirable shooting dog, the Golden today spends more time romping with the family than in the duck blind or the field. Often considered the ideal dog to hunt over, compete with or just live with and hug a lot, the Golden has something to offer the sportsman, dog fancier or professional dog lover.

The Golden Retriever can trace its ancestry back to a single breeding and the first pair of yellow retrievers destined to be called 'Golden.' The fancy is indebted to a Scotsman, the former Sir Dudley Marjoriebanks, first Lord Tweedmouth of Guisachan at Inverness, Scotland, and the first 'breeder' of our golden dog.

Typical of 19th century aristocracy, Tweedmouth was an avid sportsman and waterfowl enthusiast. His passion as a hunter was equalled only by his dedication to the sporting dog, having owned and bred Beagles, pointers, setters, Greyhounds, Scottish Deerhounds and Irish Water Spaniels.

During the 1850s he turned his attention to the moderate-sized retriever varieties who were the 'water dogs' of that era. Such dogs were known to be desirable combinations of setters and spaniels and other working varieties. They possessed great courage, strength, sagacity and temperament, and, not surprisingly, a

The colour of the Golden Retriever is any shade of gold or cream, neither mahogany nor red. They are powerful for their size and highly intelligent.

9

superior nose. Although colour was unimportant to most sportsmen, who understandably cared more about working capabilities, Tweedmouth was a true vanguard of his time and was bent on developing a yellow retriever strain.

For many years the dog fancy embraced the romantic myth that Tweedmouth had acquired his first yellow dogs from a troupe of Russian circus dogs. That 'golden' tale was dispelled by the late Elma Stonex of Somerset, England, recognised judge and breeder of the Dorcas Goldens, a noted authority on Golden Retrievers who researched and uncovered the true history of the breed.

In an article in *Dog World* magazine, Mrs. Stonex wrote of information published in 1952 and 1953 in *Country Life* magazine. Contributed by the sixth Earl of Ilchester, a noted historian and sportsman, the articles revealed the breeding records of his great-uncle, Lord Tweedmouth, from his kennel at his Guisachan estate.

Those records, dated 1835 through 1890, contain no reference to dogs of Russian origin. They indicated that Tweedmouth purchased his first yellow retriever in Brighton in 1865, a dog named Nous (the Greek word for wisdom) out of a litter of otherwise all-black Wavy-Coated Retrievers.

Golden Retrievers were developed as outdoor dogs. They were regarded as companions for the lonely hunter, assistants to bring in downed game, and handsome working animals. To this day Goldens enjoy outdoor activities more than anything.

Even though Golden Retrievers are large dogs, heavily boned and muscled, they can manoeuvre gracefully, hunt for long hours in the field and run at a rapid, sustained pace.

Recorded as bred by the Earl of Chichester, Nous is shown in photographs from 1870 to be a large and handsome dog with a very wavy medium-colour coat, very much resembling the modern Golden Retriever.

DID YOU KNOW?

Early writers spoke of the virtues of the Water Spaniel, ancestor of the Golden Retriever. 'He rushes in with the most incredible fortitude and impetuosity, through and over every obstacle that can present itself, to the execution of his office... He rivals every other breed in his attachment to his master.' Those same words easily describe the twenty-first-century Golden.

Two years later, Tweedmouth's cousin, David Robertson, presented him with a Tweed Water Spaniel named Belle. David lived at Ladykirk, which was located on the Tweed River, and the Tweed Water Spaniel was the preferred hunting dog of that region. Historians describe the Tweed Water Spaniel as 'a small English Retriever of a liver colour,' (liver meaning all shades of sandy, fawn or brown), a dog with a tightly curled coat who was an apparent descendant of the composite 'Water Dogs' of the early nineteenth century. Belle was destined to become the foundation of Tweedmouth's plan to develop a yellow retriever breed.

DID YOU KNOW?

Dogs and wolves are members of the genus *Canis*. Wolves are known scientifically as *Canis lupus* while dogs are known as *Canis domesticus*. Dogs and wolves are known to interbreed. The term canine derives from the Latin derived word *Canis*. The term **dog** has no scientific basis but has been used for thousands of years. The origin of the word **dog** has never been authoritatively ascertained.

In 1868 the now-famed breeding of Nous and Belle resulted in four yellow pups which Tweedmouth named Ada, Cowslip, Crocus and Primrose. He kept Cowslip to continue his pursuit of breeding yellow retrievers, and gave the other three pups to relatives and friends who shared his dream of producing superior yellow dogs. Ada was given to his nephew, the fifth Earl of Ilchester, who founded the Melbury line of retrievers and often crossed his yellow progeny with other Wavy-Coats and Labradors.

In 1873 Cowslip was bred to another Tweed Water Spaniel, also given by David Robertson, and Tweedmouth kept a bitch pup he named Topsy. Three years later Topsy produced Zoe, who was later bred twice to Sweep, a descendant of Ada and bred by Lord Ilchester. In 1884 Zoe whelped another litter, this time sired by Jack, another son of Cowslip, who had been sired by a red setter in 1876. This litter produced a second Nous, who is the final link between Tweedmouth's breedings and today's Golden Retriever.

Golden Retrievers are often credited with having derived from the Tweed Water Spaniel. They possess a great love of water.

PHOTO BY KENT & DONNA DANNEN

A Golden Retriever, bringing to the hunter a downed pheasant. Goldens must have 'soft mouths', which means they don't damage the game when they retrieve it.

This second Nous was bred to a dog named Queenie, who was out of Nous' sister and a black Flat-Coat sire. Two pups, Prim and Rose, no doubt named for their generations-removed ancestors, are believed to be behind the first two Golden Retrievers registered with The Kennel Club.

This last yellow litter from Nous and Queenie, recorded in 1889, shows four different lines going back to Cowslip in five generations. Linebreeding of this nature was most unusual in those days, so Tweedmouth was a true pioneer of his time.

Although reading about 'Dogs A and B' bred to 'Dogs C and D' and beyond can become somewhat tiresome, these important detailed records reveal how the Golden's yellow coat became the hallmark of the breed. The second Lord Tweedmouth followed his father's dream and bred yellow retrievers until Guisachan was sold in 1905, although sadly, he failed to keep records of his breedings.

The final connection between Tweedmouth's yellow retrievers and today's Golden pedigrees is contained in a letter to his daughter, Marjorie Lady Pentland, written by John MacLennan, one of the Guisachan keepers. MacLennan had a litter of pups from a daughter of Lady, a bitch owned by Hon. Archie Marjoriebanks, Tweedmouth's youngest son. In his letter

During the early 20th century, the Golden Retriever was referred to as the Yellow Retriever. The term *yellow* was formally dropped in 1920 in favour of the current name.

MacLennan stated he had sold two pups to the first Viscount Harcourt, founder of the famous Culham Kennel, whose dogs are behind the entire Golden Retriever breed. Those two pups are believed to be descendants of Prim and Rose and the foundation stock of the Culham line.

Lord Harcourt was a major player in those early Golden years and was the first exhibitor to show the breed in England (then known and registered as Flat-Coats, Golden) at the Crystal Palace show in 1908. His great sires, Culham Brass and Culham Copper (1905) were registered with the Kennel Club in 1903 and 1905.

In 1906 Lord Harcourt was joined in the ring by Winifred Maude Charlesworth, the most

notable of early Golden aficionados. Mrs. Charlesworth spent 50 years breeding, training and campaigning her beloved Goldens. She was the force responsible for the formation of the Golden Retriever Club in 1913, and for many years she served as Honourary Secretary for the Club. That same year, also largely due to Mrs. Charlesworth's efforts, Goldens were afforded their own category and registered as 'Yellow or Golden Retrievers.' The 'Yellow' was officially dropped in 1920.

The importance of Mrs. Charlesworth to the Golden breed is legendary among

DID YOU KNOW?

Since dogs have been inbred for centuries, their physical and mental characteristics are constantly being changed to suit man's desires for hunting, retrieving, scenting, guarding, and warming their master's laps. During the past 150 years, dogs have been judged according to physical characteristics as well as functional abilities. Few breeds can boast a genuine balance between physique, working ability and temperament.

Golden fanciers. Under the prefix of Normanby (later changed to Noranby) her breedings to Lord Harcourt's famous sires appear in every Golden Retriever pedigree today. She was a dynamic personality, and her dedication to the breed established the Golden as a premier gundog in the British retriever world. Active in field trials as well as conformation, Mrs. Charlesworth was dedicated to the preservation of the working Golden who combined both type and soundness. Her dogs were sound and powerfully built, with lovely heads, and took honours on the bench and in the field. Her energy and

DID YOU KNOW?

Yellow pups occasionally appear in litters of all-black retrievers. The colour is due to a recessive gene. Such deviation from the normal pattern is considered a mutation, and the resulting yellow pup is called a 'sport.'

enthusiasm in both venues promoted the Golden as a most capable gundog who was competitive with the other retrievers of that time. In her 1933 book, she credits Lord Tweedmouth as instrumental in obtaining her first Golden, Normanby Beauty, which leads the reader to assume that bitch was directly from a Tweedmouth breeding.

Whether you are considering a Golden Retriever as a pet, show dog, field worker or competition dog, the breed is amongst the most handsome of all purebred dogs.

One of the Golden Retriever's most admired characteristics is its water repellent undercoat, which essentially keeps the skin dry thus making the dog more buoyant.

Beauty's first litters were all by Culham sires. Many of those offspring...Normanby Balfour, Chs. Noranby Campfire (the first Golden ever to win a bench title), Noranby Daydawn, Noranby Jeptha, Noranby Diana, Noranby Dutiful and Noranby Dierdre, Ch.-F.T.Ch. Noranby Destiny...are influential ancestors in the breed. Mrs. Charlesworth was well into her seventies when Destiny rose to her dual championship in 1950.

In the early 1900s, retrievers of all colours competed in the field trial meets. In 1904 the International Gundog League Open Stake was won by a 'liver Flat-Coat' who was recorded as sired by Lord Tweedmouth's Golden Flat-Coat Lucifer, an accomplishment heralded by some historians as possibly the first Golden Retriever field trial win. The important fact remains that most Goldens of that era who competed on the bench also took honours in the field. Bench champions

DID YOU KNOW?

In India, a six-year-old police-trained Golden Retriever named Madhu (the Indian word for honey) was used to guard the palace grounds and home of the late Prime Minister Nehru.

often earned field trial placements or Certificates of Merit (commenda-tions for excellent work), and the breed was enormously popular as hunting partners in the shooting community. Although they were not noted for being 'fast,' they were known for

Golden Retriever puppies are very playful and mischievous. Few can resist the charms and antics of a pair of Golden pups. They usually mature mentally when they are about two years old.

their excellent water ability as well as superb biddability and temperament. Those same characteristics describe the Golden Retriever of the 21st century.

Championship shows and field trials came to an abrupt halt during the Second World War, with only a few breeders maintaining quality lines. Pet breeding prospered, however, in the post-war years, and the number of registered Golden Retrievers increased steadily every year. By the 1990s, Goldens numbered fourth in total Kennel Club breed registrations.

Today Goldens arrive in great numbers at Championship Shows, and it is not unusual to find several hundred Golden Retriever entries at one show. Entry size often requires a separate judge for dogs and bitches.

Golden popularity contin-ues to spread worldwide. In many countries Goldens must meet a certain standard before they can be registered with the national kennel club. Some countries also require that a Golden Retriever demonstrate some measurable degree of retrieving talent before they can be declared a champion on the bench. The American Kennel Club requires only that the sire and dam be registered in order for their puppies to qualify for registration, a process which does not ensure the ongoing quality of the breed. In too many instances, breeders are more interested in profit than in producing puppies that are representative of their breed.

Retrieving and swimming come as naturally to a Golden Retriever as being a devoted companion dog. Here a Golden Retriever fetches a downed duck.

Golden Retriever

It might be apropos to call the Golden Retriever the 'golden treasure at the rainbow's end.' As the ideal all-around companion and sporting dog, the Golden offers something for every person or inclination. Tweedmouth's masterful linebreeding cemented the superb qualities of his yellow retrievers and, many generations later, Goldens remain the most versatile of the retriever breeds. Supremely intelligent and blessedly trainable, they also remain as devoted to their masters as the dogs of yore. Their talent is without equal, and the modern Golden excels in every canine discipline, including simple household amusements such as stick-fetch and shoe and sock theft. The Golden's disposition is as sunny as his outer coat, and he is considered by many to be the perfect family dog, the ideal companion for all ages and activities.

While the Golden Retriever may be the ideal dog, not every person is an ideal owner. You may love dogs and have a soft spot for the Golden, but love alone is not enough. Consider the big picture before you add a Golden to your household.

If you want to keep your Golden Retriever looking as beautiful as this dog, you must be prepared for the daily grooming and exercising of your pet.

SIZE

The Golden is a medium-to-large size dog who requires a good bit of space indoors and out. Everything about the dog is big, including his hairy paws, which will track mud and dirt onto your kitchen floor. His happy wagging tail will sweep your prized glassware from low-standing table tops. His natural curiosity will lead to rows of nose prints on the glass above your windowsills. Given a single opportunity, he will claim at least two couch cushions or your easy chair. A fenced garden or large-sized kennel run is a must to safely confine and exercise a large and energetic Golden Retriever.

Goldens thrive on fun activities with their owners. Few breeds demand as much time and energy from the owners as the Golden Retriever. This fellow is ready for more!

COAT CARE

Part of the Golden Retriever's universal appeal is his lovely golden coat. Although a wide variety exists in length, texture and colour, the golden coat is still his most distinguishing character-istic. Colours range from very pale cream to gold, but excludes dark red or mahogany shades. The lighter shades are more common in the show ring, with proponents of the darker golden passionately dedicated to their colour prefer-ence. Most coats are straight to slightly wavy and of medium length, although longer coats also are more common on the bench. Coat colour also has no bearing on intelligence, temperament or ability. Professional grooming is an option, but if you decide to use a grooming service, investigate the cost and be sure you can handle that expense.

TIME AND EXERCISE

The biddable personality of the Golden Retriever is no accident. His strong work ethic and desire to please were traits important to Lord Tweedmouth and were paramount in his yellow strain of dogs. As a gentle, friendly dog with a most forgiving disposition, the Golden wishes only to make his owner happy. He will not thrive in solitude and needs to live as part of his family unit.

Goldens are also natural athletes who are joyful workers and willing to try any sport or physical activity as long as there is a human at the other end. These are energetic dogs who

> **DID YOU KNOW?**
> As if one coat isn't enough, Goldens are a 'double-coated' breed, possessing an outer coat of long silky guard hairs and a soft downy undercoat that insulates the dog from temperature extremes, an important characteristic in a dog who must retrieve birds, especially waterfowl, under all weather conditions.

The two photos above show normal Golden Retriever hairs magnified 60-150 times their actual size.
The two lower photos show distressed hairs that are smashed (right) or frayed (left).

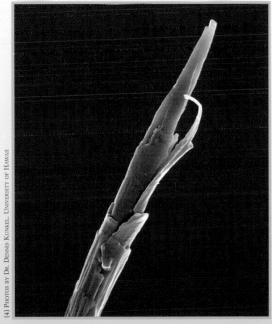

require exercise and an active lifestyle to channel their enthusiasm in the right direction. A play area is not enough. Your Golden will not exercise without you. YOU are his reason to run, walk or play. You must commit to at least one good walk each day plus daily games of fetch, Frisbee games or bumper chasing (those large, canvas rolls sold in pet shops and pet supply catalogues for retrieve-a-holic dogs). Daily exercise periods will keep your Golden physically fit and stimulated and too tired to entertain himself destructively. Exercise is also a natural canine (and human!) stress reliever and will help prevent symptoms of separation anxiety and other stress-related behaviours from occurring.

DID YOU KNOW?

The Golden coat can also create problems for the hunter who must comb out seeds, burrs and tangled twigs after a long day in the field.

Although most Goldens are energetic adolescents, some lines of show dogs produce more laid-back pups with lower energy requirements. If your canine companion goal is a Golden couch potato, research breeders who do not stress the working aspects of the breed. Be sure the puppy's parents are calm individuals both indoors and out; scrutinise their response to play activities. Check the breeder's references and past puppy owners to learn more about the temperaments of other pups.

Goldens can be highly trained as hunting dogs. They also can be trained to respond to various whistle commands, in addition to hand signals and verbal commands.

Good research should produce puppies you will enjoy living with.

DISCIPLINE

Even laid-back Golden Retriever puppies will require training to learn the rules of their new human world. Although highly trainable, Goldens are not born already trained, a surprise to some new owners who expect their Golden puppy to behave like the model Golden citizens they see on television. Good manners are not included in his purchase price. It is up to you to teach your Golden acceptable behaviour in your home and in your neighbourhood. That means weekly obedience classes with an experienced instructor and practice sessions with your Golden every day. If you

cannot or will not commit to the time constraints of puppy training, perhaps you should rethink your decision to get this dog.

ORAL FIXATION

As a breed, Goldens are very oral dogs; after all, let us not forget their retrieving heritage. From pup to senior, most Goldens love, indeed they need, to have something in their mouth. It does not matter if that object is a toy, a table leg or your left hand. What is important is that this dog loves and needs to chew.

One of your major puppy challenges is teaching your puppy what he may or may not put between his tiny teeth. That will take effort, time and patience, but your pup is worth all that and more. Read the training section on techniques to discourage inappropriate chewing. If by four or five months of age your pup still chews destructively, seek the help of a professional canine behaviourist. The dog may in fact be fine, and the problem might be you.

This Golden puppy didn't know that digging up the garden is forbidden. Proactive training is a must with Golden puppies. Be certain your pup understands all the household rules.

DID YOU KNOW?
A Golden Retriever's nose may turn slightly pink during long periods of very cold weather. Called a 'snow nose,' the discolouration is normal and the nose will return to black when warm weather returns. The colour of the nose leather sometimes fades in older dogs and may become pinkish brown as the dog ages.

23

NOT QUITE A GUARD DOG

Given all the people-friendly qualities of the breed, it is no surprise most Goldens fail as guard dogs. The typical Golden might lick a home invader to death, which is not protection at its best. Goldens can be encouraged to give a warning bark, but their wildly wagging tail is a dead give-away.

However, despite their ingrained friendly attitude, give up the family silver, they also trust their dogs would rise to their personal defence.

THE GOLDEN'S NATURAL APTITUDES

OBEDIENCE AND AGILITY

As sporting dogs, Goldens are naturally athletic. They are also very trainable and obedient. Therefore, it is no surprise to see a large entry of Goldens in obedience competition and

The ever-friendly Golden Retriever makes a far better guide dog and hunting dog than he could ever make a guard dog. This young pup has a bright future ahead of him.

stories abound about Goldens who have sensed danger to their families, especially their children, and reacted to protect them. Whilst most Goldens owners believe their dogs would agility trials. Depending on how much advanced training you want to do with your Golden, these are areas in which the Golden excels and may be of interest to the Golden owner.

GUIDE DOGS AND ASSISTANCE WORK

The people-loving Golden Retriever is ideally suited for assistance work. Particularly attuned to human needs and emotions, they are eager and willing students who are easily trained for the complex tasks involved in guide and service work. There are organisations that enlist puppy-raisers who raise and socialise Golden youngsters until 12 months of age, when they return to guide dog school for advanced training and placement. Recipients who have had other breed guide dogs before their Golden Retriever speak high praise of their Golden's devotion and desire to please when compared to their former canine helpers.

THERAPY

Golden Retrievers excel as therapy dogs for the same reasons they do well in service work; they are uniquely sensitive to human needs and feelings. In hospitals, senior centres and nursing homes, Goldens continue to prove the power of a friendly paw or velvet muzzle on the knee.

Golden Retrievers and their owners frequently participate in field trials. Goldens are naturally obedient, intelligent and very trainable.

PHOTO COURTESY OF THE SEEING EYE®, MORRISTOWN, NJ USA

Thousands of Goldens are trained as guide dogs for the visually impaired with dignity and devotion.

25

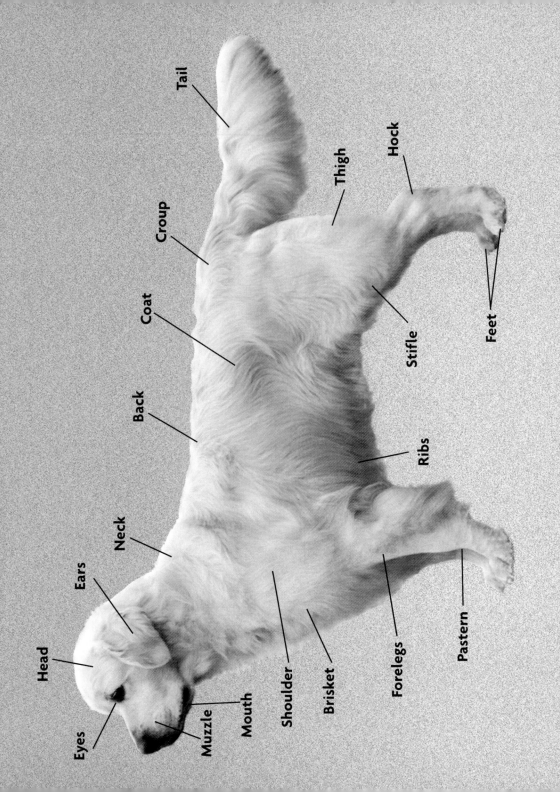

BREED STANDARD FOR THE
Golden Retriever

In order to appreciate, select and understand a proper Golden Retriever puppy or adult, it's important to also understand The Kennel Club standard for the breed. Breed standards are the guidelines which have for decades preserved the qualities that define each breed of dog. They have been developed to protect and advance the soundness, temperament, natural ability and personality reflected in those qualities. The Golden Retriever Club adheres to the foundation laid by Tweedmouth, Nous and Belle. Such is the responsibility of every breed's parent club in its goals to preserve the purity of its breed.

Without a fixed standard or guideline, one could breed a Golden with a flat face, prick ears or speckled coat to another dog with equally un-golden characteristics, and a generation or two down the road, you'd have a Golden who looked more like a terrier or a bulldog.

Although such examples are extreme, a breed as populous as the Golden is bound to experience some degree of indiscriminate breeding. If you know the ideal Golden's qualities, you will be able to recognise and choose a decent Golden puppy to suit your personal and competitive goals.

THE KENNEL CLUB STANDARD FOR THE GOLDEN RETRIEVER
General Appearance:
Symmetrical, balanced, active, powerful, level mover, sound with kindly expression.

Characteristics: Biddable, intelligent and possessing natural working ability.

Temperament: Kindly, friendly and confident.

Head and Skull: Balanced and well chiselled, skull broad without coarseness; well set on

The desired head of the Golden Retriever is well-chiselled and never coarse.

neck, muzzle powerful, wide and deep. Length of foreface approximately equals length from well-defined stop to occiput. Nose black.

Eyes: Dark brown, set well apart, dark rims.

Ears: Moderate size, set on approximately level with eyes.

Mouth: Jaws strong, with perfect, regular and complete scissor bite, i.e., upper teeth closely overlapping lower teeth and set to the jaws.

Study the breed standard to understand your Golden Retriever's anatomy.

Neck: Good length, clean and muscular.

Forequarters: Forelegs straight with good bone, shoulders well laid back, long in blade with upper arm of equal length placing legs well under body. Elbows close fitting.

Body: Balanced, short coupled, deep through heart. Ribs well sprung. Level topline.

Hindquarters: Loin and legs strong and muscular, good second thighs, well bent stifles (knees). Hocks (lower rear legs above the

foot) well let down, straight when viewed from rear, neither turning in nor out. Cow hocks (rear legs bending inward toward each other) highly undesirable.

Feet: Round and cat-like.

Tail: Set on and carried level with back, reaching to hocks, without curl at top.

Gait/Movement: Powerful with good drive. Straight and true in front and rear. Stride long and free with no sign of hackney action in front.

Coat: Flat or wavy with good feathering, dense water resisting undercoat.

Colour: Any shade of gold or cream, neither red nor mahogany. A few white hairs on chest only permissible.

Size: Height at withers; Dogs 56-61 cms (22-24 ins); Bitches 51-56 cms (20-22 ins).

Faults: Any departure from the foregoing points should be considered a fault and the seriousness with which the fault should be regarded should be in exact proportion to its degree.

Note: Male animal should have two apparently normal testicles fully descended into the scrotum.

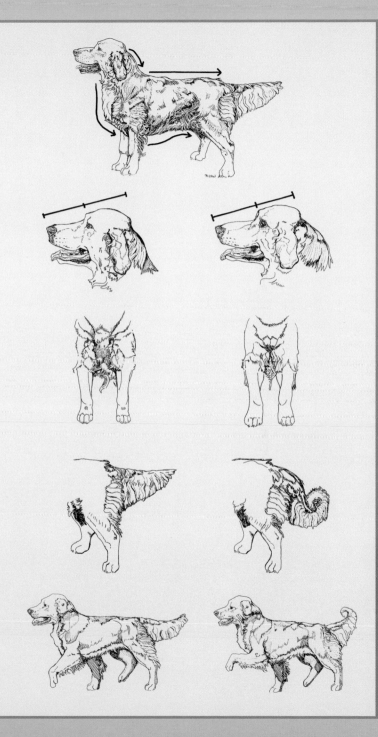

BODY

The body must be symmetrical and balanced.

HEAD

The foreface approximately equals the length from stop to occiput.

FORELEGS

The forelegs straight and the shoulders well laid back.

TAIL

The tail carried level with back, never curling at the top.

GAIT

Stride long and free with no sign of hackney action.

Finding a healthy, happy Golden puppy from an experienced breeder is the best path for the new owner. This pup is from Gold-Rush Kennels.

Golden Retriever

WHERE TO BEGIN?

If you are convinced that the Golden Retriever is the ideal dog for you, it is time to learn about where to find a puppy and what to look for. Locating a litter of Golden Retrievers should not present a problem for the new owner. You should inquire about breeders in your area who enjoy a good reputation in the breed. You are looking for an established breeder with outstanding dog ethics and a strong commitment to the breed. New owners should have as many questions as they have doubts. An established breeder is indeed the one to answer your four million questions and make you comfortable with your choice of the Golden Retriever. An established breeder will sell you a puppy at a fair price if, and only if, the breeder determines that you are a suitable, worthy owner of his/her dogs. An established breeder can be relied upon for advice, no matter what time of day or night. A reputable breeder will accept a puppy back, without questions, should you decide that this not the right dog for you.

When choosing a breeder, reputation is much more important than convenience of location. Do not be overly impressed by breeders who run brag advertisements in the presses about their stupendous champions and working lines. The real quality breeders are quiet and unassuming. You hear about them at the dog trials and shows, by word of mouth. You may be well advised to avoid the novice who lives only a couple miles away. The local novice breeder,

DID YOU KNOW?

If you lead an erratic, unpredictable life, with daily or weekly changes in your work requirements, consider the problems of owning a puppy. The new puppy has to be fed regularly, socialised (loved, petted, handled, introduced to other people) and, most importantly, allowed to visit outdoors for toilet training. As the dog gets older, it can be more tolerant of deviations in its feeding and toilet relief.

trying so hard to get rid of that first litter of puppies, is more than accommodating and anxious to sell you one. That breeder will charge you as much as any established breeder. The novice breeder is not going to interrogate you and your family about your

Before meeting with the breeder, be clear about what your intentions for your Golden Retriever will be. You cannot buy a Golden for a pet and later decide that you want to show him.

intentions with the puppy, the environment and training you can provide, etc. That breeder will be nowhere to be found when your poorly bred, badly adjusted four-pawed monster starts to growl and spit up at midnight or eat the family cat!

Socialisation is a breeder concern of immense importance. Since the Golden Retriever's temperament can vary from line to line, socialisation is the first and best way to encourage a proper, stable personality.

Choosing a breeder is an important first step in dog ownership. Fortunately, the majority of Golden Retriever

breeders are devoted to the breed and its well being. New owners should have little problem finding a reputable breeder who does not live on the other side of the country (or in a different country). The Kennel Club is able to recommend breeders of quality Golden Retrievers, as can any local all-breed club or Golden Retriever club. Potential owners are encouraged to attend dog shows and obedience

Making a choice of which Golden puppy is best for you depends upon your definition of what you expect in a Golden. A show dog requires brains and beauty; a hunting dog requires stamina, trainability and musculature; a pet requires personality and soundness. The choice is not simple.

trials to see the Golden Retrievers in action; to get an idea what Golden Retrievers look like outside of a photographer's lens. Provided you approach the handlers when they are not terribly busy with the dogs, most are more than willing to answer questions, recommend breeders and give advice.

Now that you have contacted and met a breeder or two and made your choice about which breeder is best suited to your needs, it is time to visit the litter. Keep in mind that many top breeders have waiting lists. Sometimes new owners have to wait as long as two years for a puppy. If you are really committed to the breeder whom you have selected, then you will wait (and hope for an early arrival!). If not, you may have to resort to your second or third choice

breeder. Do not be too anxious, however. If the breeder does not have any waiting list, or any customers, there is probably a good reason. It is no different than visiting a pub with no clientele. The better pubs and restaurants always have a waiting list and it is usually worth the wait. Besides, is not a puppy more important than a pint?

DID YOU KNOW?
Breeders rarely release puppies until they are eight to ten weeks of age. This is an acceptable age for most breeds of dog, excepting toy breeds which are not released until around 12 weeks, given their petite sizes. If a breeder has a puppy that is 12 weeks or more, it is likely well socialised and housetrained. Be sure that it is otherwise healthy before deciding to take it home.

Since you are likely choosing a Golden Retriever as a pet dog and not a working dog, you simply should select a pup that is friendly and attractive. While the basic structure of the breed has little variation, the temperament may present trouble in certain strains. Beware of the shy or overly aggressive puppy: be

Bring the family along to assist in the selection. Some puppies are attracted to some individuals in your family. It could be instinct, fate or merely someone's perfume or cologne.

especially conscious of the nervous Golden Retriever pup. Do not let sentiment or emotion trap you into buying the runt of the litter.

The gender of your puppy is largely a matter of personal taste, although there is a common

> **DID YOU KNOW?**
> Some experts in canine health advise that stress during a dog's early years of development can compromise and weaken his immune system and may trigger the potential for a shortened life expectancy. They emphasize the need for happy and stress-free growing-up years.

> **DID YOU KNOW?**
> If the breeder from whom you are buying a puppy asks you a lot of personal questions, do not be insulted. Such a breeder wants to be sure that you will be a fit provider for his puppy.

belief amongst those who work with Golden Retrievers that bitches are quicker to learn and generally more loving and faithful. Males learn more slowly but retain the lesson longer. The difference in size is noticeable but slight.

Breeders commonly allow visitors to see the litter by around the fifth or sixth week, and puppies leave for their new homes between the eighth and tenth week. Breeders who permit their puppies to leave early are more interested in your pounds than their puppies' well being. Puppies need to learn the rules of the trade from their dams, and most dams continue teaching the pups manners and dos and don'ts until around the eighth week. Breeders spend significant amounts of time with the Golden Retriever toddlers so that they are able to interact with the 'other species,' i.e., humans. Given the long history that dogs and humans have, bonding between the two species is natural but must be nurtured. A well-bred, well-socialised Golden Retriever pup wants

adjust to life together. If you have observed a litter in action, you have obtained a firsthand look at the dynamics of a puppy 'pack' and, thus, you should learn about each pup's individual personality—perhaps you have even found one that particularly appeals to you.

However, even if you have not yet found the Golden Retriever puppy of your dreams,

When you buy a Golden Retriever puppy you should get a copy of the registration and the pedigree. The breeder should be able to answer all your questions about her kennel, health concerns and the breed in general.

nothing more than to be near you and please you.

COMMITMENT OF OWNERSHIP

After considering all of these factors, you have most likely already made some very important decisions about selecting your puppy. You have chosen a Golden Retriever, which means that you have decided which characteristics you want in a dog and what type of dog will best fit into your family and lifestyle. If you have selected a breeder, you have gone a step further—you have done your research and found a responsible, conscientious person who breeds quality Golden Retriever and who should be a reliable source of help as you and your puppy

DID YOU KNOW?

Two important documents you will get from the breeder are the pup's pedigree and registration papers. The breeder should register the litter and each pup with The Kennel Club, and it is necessary for you to have the paperwork if you plan on showing or breeding in the future.

Make sure you know the breeder's intentions on which type of registration he will obtain for the pup. There are limited registrations which may prohibit the dog from being shown or from competing in non-conformation trials such as Working or Agility if the breeder feels that the pup is not of sufficient quality to do so. There is also a type of registration that will permit the dog in non-conformation competition only.

If your dog is registered with a Kennel-Club-recognised breed club, then you can register the pup with The Kennel Club yourself. Your breeder can assist you with the specifics of the registration process.

35

Golden Retrievers typically have large litters, sometimes as many as a dozen puppies. Potential buyers have many adorable contestants to review.

observing pups will help you learn to recognise certain behaviour and to determine what a pup's behaviour indicates about his temperament. You will be able to pick out which pups are the leaders, which ones are less outgoing, which ones are confident, which ones are shy, playful, friendly, aggressive, etc. Equally as important, you will learn to recognise what a healthy pup should look and act like. All of these things will help you in your search, and when you find the Golden Retriever that was meant for you, you will know it!

Researching your breed, selecting a responsible breeder and observing as many pups as possible are all important steps on the way to dog ownership. It may seem like a lot of effort...and you have not even taken the pup home yet! Remember, though, you cannot be too careful when it comes to deciding on the type of dog you want and finding out about your prospective pup's background.

DID YOU KNOW?

Your puppy should have a well-fed appearance but not a distended abdomen, which may indicate worms or incorrect feeding, or both. The body should be firm, with a solid feel. The skin of the abdomen should be pale pink and clean, without signs of scratching or rash. Check the hind legs to make certain that dewclaws were removed, if any were present at birth.

Buying a puppy is not—or should not be—just another whimsical purchase. This is one instance in which you actually do get to choose your own family! You may be thinking that buying a puppy should be fun—it should not be so serious and so much work. Keep in mind that your puppy is not a cuddly stuffed toy or decorative lawn ornament, but a creature that will become a real member of your family. You will come to realise that, whilst buying a puppy is a pleasurable and exciting endeavour, it is not something to be taken lightly. Relax…the fun will start when the pup comes home!

Always keep in mind that a puppy is nothing more than a baby in a furry disguise…a baby who is virtually helpless in a human world and who trusts his owner for fulfilment of his basic needs for survival. In addition to water and shelter, your pup needs care, protection, guidance and love. If you are not prepared to commit to this, then you are not prepared to own a dog.

You should think long-term when you consider buying a dog of any breed. Food, veterinary care, training, possibly doggie day care, are short-term as well as lifetime expenses and will seriously impact your budget. You must allow for your pup's initial veterinary care as well as

Don't forget that you are not buying a stuffed doll. With ownership comes responsibility. Your Golden puppy will depend upon you for food, shelter, training and companionship.

the future and ongoing costs of routine shots and check-ups, spaying/neutering, possible emergency care and medications for the inevitable canine illnesses your dog may experience. And as with a sick child, canine emergencies need attention now, not later when you collect a bonus or commission.

Wait a minute, you say. How hard could this be? All of my neighbours own dogs and they seem to be doing just fine. Why

---

DID YOU KNOW?

Many good breeders will offer you insurance with your new puppy, which is an excellent idea. The first few weeks of insurance will probably be covered free of charge or with only minimal cost, allowing you to take up the policy when this expires. If you own a pet dog, it is sensible to take out such a policy as veterinary fees can be high, although routine vaccinations and boosters are not covered. Look carefully at the many options open to you before deciding which suits best.

37

should I have to worry about all of this? Well, you should not worry about it; in fact, you will probably find that once your Golden Retriever pup gets used to his new home, he will fall into his place in the family quite naturally. But it never hurts to emphasise the commitment of dog ownership. With some time and patience, it is really not too difficult to raise a curious and exuberant Golden Retriever pup to be a well-adjusted and well-mannered adult dog—a dog that could be your most loyal friend.

Unless you want to enter dog shows, you do not need a show dog. Get a pet-quality Golden from a reputable breeder.

PREPARING PUPPY'S PLACE IN YOUR HOME

Researching your breed and finding a breeder are only two aspects of the 'homework' you will have to do before bringing

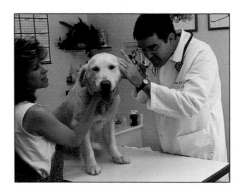

your Golden Retriever puppy home. You will also have to prepare your home and family for the new addition. Much like you would prepare a nursery for a newborn baby, you will need to designate a place in your home that will be the puppy's own. How you prepare your home will depend on how much freedom the dog will be allowed. Will he be confined to one room or a specific area in the house, or will he be allowed to roam as he pleases? Will he spend most of his time in the house or will he be primarily an outdoor dog? Whatever you decide, you must ensure that he has a place that he can 'call his own.'

When you bring your new puppy into your home, you are bringing him into what will become his home as well. Obviously, you did not buy a puppy so that he could take over your house, but in order for a puppy to grow into a stable, well-adjusted dog, he

DID YOU KNOW?

An important consideration to be discussed is the sex of your puppy. For a family companion, a bitch may be the better choice, considering the female's inbred concern for all young creatures and her accompanying tolerance and patience. It is always advised to spay a pet bitch, which may guarantee her a longer life.

WHAT YOU SHOULD BUY
CRATE

To someone unfamiliar with the use of crates in dog training, it may seem like punishment to shut a dog in a crate, but this is not the case at all. Crates are not cruel—crates have many humane and highly effective uses in dog care and training. For example, crate training is a very popular and very successful housebreaking method. A crate can keep your dog safe during travel; and,

You have just brought your Golden Retriever puppy home. Are you prepared for the first night? Have you obtained the necessities?

has to feel comfortable in his surroundings. Remember, he is leaving the warmth and security of his mother and littermates, as well as the familiarity of the only place he has ever known, so it is important to make his transition as easy as possible. By preparing a place in your home for the puppy, you are making him feel as welcome as possible in a strange new place. It should not take him long to get used to it, but the sudden shock of being transplanted is somewhat traumatic for a young pup. Imagine how a small child would feel in the same situation—that is how your puppy must be feeling. It is up to you to reassure him and to let him know, 'Little fellow, you are going to like it here!'

DID YOU KNOW?
Unfortunately, when a puppy is bought by someone who does not take into consideration the time and attention that dog ownership requires, it is the puppy who suffers when he is either abandoned or placed in a shelter by a frustrated owner. So all of the 'homework' you do in preparation for your pup's arrival will benefit you both. The more informed you are, the more you will know what to expect and the better equipped you will be to handle the ups and downs of raising a puppy. Hopefully, everyone in the household is willing to do his part in raising and caring for the pup. The anticipation of owning a dog often brings a lot of promises from excited family members: 'I will walk him every day,' 'I will feed him,' 'I will housebreak him,' etc., but these things take time and effort, and promises can easily be forgotten once the novelty of the new pet has worn off.

39

No creature is more impressionable than a young Golden Retriever. Embark on your pup's training with kindness and consistency and you will be rewarded with an obedient companion.

something a little more luxurious than leaves and twigs lining a dirty ditch.

As far as purchasing a crate, the type that you buy is up to you. It will most likely be one of the two most popular types: wire or fibreglass. There are advantages and disadvantages to each type. For example, a wire crate is more open, allowing the air to flow through and affording the dog a view of what is going on around him. A fibreglass crate, however, is sturdier and can double as a travel crate since it provides more protection for the dog. The size of the crate is another thing to consider. Puppies do not stay puppies forever—in fact, sometimes it seems as if they grow right before your eyes. A Yorkie-sized crate may be fine for a very young Golden Retriever pup, but it will not do him much good for long! Unless you have the money and the inclination to buy a

perhaps most importantly, a crate provides your dog with a place of his own in your home. It serves as a 'doggie bedroom' of sorts—your Golden Retriever can curl up in his crate when he wants to sleep or when he just needs a break. Many dogs sleep in their crates overnight. When lined with soft blankets and filled with his favourite toys, a crate becomes a cosy pseudo-den for your dog. Like his ancestors, he too will seek out the comfort and retreat of a den—you just happen to be providing him with

DID YOU KNOW?
Never house your Golden puppy in a kennel run with gravel or similar flooring. Golden puppies are notorious chewers and will happily dine on small, loose stones. Veterinary surgeons' stories abound about puppies who are presented for emergency surgery because they have ingested objects thought to be impossible to swallow.

new crate every time your pup has a growth spurt, it is better to get one that will accommodate your dog both as a pup and at full size. A medium-size crate will be necessary for a full-grown Golden Retriever, who stands approximately 21 inches high.

BEDDING

A blanket or two in the dog's crate will help the dog feel more at home. First, the blankets will take the place of the leaves, twigs, etc., that the pup would use in the wild to make a den; the pup can make his own 'burrow' in the crate. Although your pup is far removed from his den-making ancestors, the denning instinct is still a part of his genetic makeup. Second, until you bring your pup home, he has been sleeping amidst the warmth of his mother and litter-mates, and whilst a blanket is not the same as a warm, breathing body, it still provides heat and something with which to snuggle. You will want to wash your pup's blankets frequently in case he has an accident in his crate, and replace or remove any blanket that becomes ragged and starts to fall apart.

TOYS

Toys are a must for dogs of all ages, especially for curious playful pups. Puppies are the

PHOTO COURTESY OF MIKKI PET PRODUCTS.

Many top breeders recommend the use of a crate in training. Your local pet shop should have a full range of dog crates from which you can select the size and colour of your preference.

'children' of the dog world, and what child does not love toys? Chew toys provide enjoyment to both dog and owner—your dog will enjoy playing with his favourite toys, whilst you will enjoy the fact that they distract him from your expensive shoes and leather sofa. Puppies love to chew; in fact, chewing is a physical need for pups as they are teething, and everything looks appetising! The full range of your possessions—from old dishrag to Oriental rug—are fair

PHOTO COURTESY OF MIKKI PET PRODUCTS

Your local pet shop will have a wide assortment of dog toys. Do not offer your dog toys designed for children. Human toys can be dangerous because they are usually too soft and may contain dangerous dyes.

DID YOU KNOW?

During crate training, you should partition off the section of the crate in which the pup stays. If he is given too big an area, this will hinder your training efforts. Crate training is based on the fact that a dog does not like to soil his sleeping quarters, so it is ineffective to keep a pup in a crate that is so big that he can eliminate in one end and get far enough away from it to sleep. Also, you want to make the crate den-like for the pup. Blankets and a favourite toy will make the crate cosy for the small pup; as he grows, you may want to evict some of his 'roommates' to make more room.

game in the eyes of a teething pup. Puppies are not all that discerning when it comes to finding something to literally 'sink their teeth into'—everything tastes great!

Golden Retriever puppies are fairly aggressive chewers and only the hardest, strongest toys should be offered to them. Breeders advise owners to resist stuffed toys, because they can become de-stuffed in no time. The overly excited pup may ingest the stuffing, which is neither digestible nor nutritious.

Similarly, squeaky toys are quite popular, but must be

DID YOU KNOW?

It will take at least two weeks for your puppy to become accustomed to his new surroundings. Give him lots of love, attention, handling, frequent opportunities to relieve himself, a diet he likes to eat and a place he can call his own.

avoided for the Golden Retriever. Perhaps a squeaky toy can be used as an aid in training, but not for free play. If a pup 'disembowels' one of these, the small plastic squeaker inside can be dangerous if swallowed. Monitor the condition of all your pup's toys carefully and get rid

The retriever breeds are the most oral of all dogs. Whilst a young pup's nip is harmless, an owner must discourage such behaviour at once.

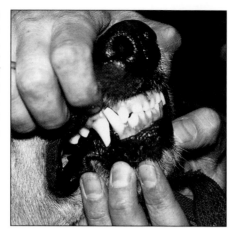

Golden Retrievers have very strong, sharp teeth that are capable of destroying most ordinary toys. Offer safe chew toys to your dog.

of any that have been chewed to the point of becoming potentially dangerous.

Be careful of natural bones, which have a tendency to splinter into sharp, dangerous pieces. Also be careful of rawhide, which can turn into pieces that are easy to swallow or into a mushy mess on your carpet.

LEAD

A nylon lead is probably the best option as it is the most resistant to puppy teeth should your pup take a liking to chewing on his lead. Of course, this is a habit that should be nipped in the bud, but if your pup likes to chew on his lead he has a very slim chance of being able to chew through the strong nylon. Nylon leads are also lightweight, which is good for a young Golden Retriever who is just getting used to the idea of

walking on a lead. For everyday walking and safety purposes, the nylon lead is a good choice. As your pup grows up and gets used to walking on the lead, you may want to purchase a flexible lead. These leads allow you to extend the length to give the dog a broader area to explore or to shorten the length to keep the close to you. Of course there are special leads for training purposes, and specially made leather harnesses for the working Golden Retrievers, but these are not necessary for routine walks.

COLLAR

Your pup should get used to wearing a collar all the time since you will want to attach his ID tags to it. You have to attach the lead to something! A lightweight nylon collar is a good

DID YOU KNOW?

The majority of problems that are commonly seen in young pups will disappear as your dog gets older. However, how you deal with problems when he is young will determine how he reacts to discipline as an adult dog. It is important to establish who is boss (hopefully it will be you!) right away when you are first bonding wiith your dog. This bond will set the tone for the rest of your life together.

choice; make sure that it fits snugly enough so that the pup cannot wriggle out of it, but is loose enough so that it will not be uncomfortably tight around the pup's neck. You should be able to fit a finger between the pup and the collar. It may take some time for your pup to get used to wearing the collar, but soon he will not even notice that it is there. Choke collars are made for training, but should only be used by an experienced handler.

FOOD AND WATER BOWLS

Your pup will need two bowls, one for food and one for water. You may want two sets of bowls, one for inside and one for outside, depending on where the dog will be fed and where he will be spending most of his time. Stainless steel or sturdy plastic bowls are popular choices. Plastic bowls are more chewable. Dogs tend not to chew on the steel variety, which can be sterilised. It is important to buy sturdy bowls since anything is in danger of being chewed by puppy teeth and you do not want your dog to be constantly chewing apart his bowl (for his safety and for your purse!).

CLEANING SUPPLIES

Until a pup is housetrained you will be doing a lot of cleaning. Accidents will occur, which is okay in the beginning because the puppy does not know any better. All you can do is be prepared to clean up any 'accidents.' Old rags, towels, newspapers and a safe disinfectant are good to have on hand.

Puppies learn from watching. If you are bringing a second dog into the household, the puppy will follow the older dog's example—a great aid in lead training and lots more.

BEYOND THE BASICS

The items previously discussed are the bare necessities. You will find out what else you need as you go along—grooming supplies, flea/tick protection, baby gates to partition a room, etc. These things will vary depending on your situation but it is important that you have everything you need to feed and make your Golden Retriever comfortable in his first few days at home.

PUPPY-PROOFING YOUR HOME

Aside from making sure that your Golden Retriever will be comfortable in your home, you also have to make sure that your

home is safe for your Golden Retriever. This means taking precautions that your pup will not get into anything he should not get into and that there is nothing within his reach that may harm him should he sniff it, chew it, inspect it, etc. This probably seems obvious since, whilst you are primarily concerned with your pup's safety, at the same time you do not want your belongings to be ruined. Breakables should be placed out of reach if your dog is to have full run of the house. If he is to be limited to certain places within the house, keep any potentially dangerous items in the 'off-limits' areas. An electrical cord can pose a danger should the puppy decide to taste it—and who is going to convince a pup that it would not make a

You should always clean up after your dog. Pet shops sell special tools that enable you to perform this essential service as simply as possible.

great chew toy? Cords should be fastened tightly against the wall. If your dog is going to spend time in a crate, make sure that there is nothing near his crate that he can reach if he sticks his curious little nose or paws through the openings. Just as you would with a child, keep all household cleaners and chemicals where the pup cannot get to them.

It is also important to make sure that the outside of your home is safe. Of course your puppy should never be unsupervised,

DID YOU KNOW?

Thoroughly puppy-proof your house before bringing your puppy home. Never use roach or rodent poisons in any area accessible to the puppy. Avoid the use of toilet bowl cleaners. Most dogs are born with toilet bowl sonar and will take a drink if the lid is left open. Also keep the trash secured and out of reach.

PHOTO COURTESY OF MIKKI PET PRODUCTS

Stainless steel water and food bowls are long lasting, though expensive. Plastic bowls are acceptable, though dogs tend to chew on them.

Your local pet shop probably carries an extensive line of food and water bowls made from hard plastic, metal and pottery.

but a pup let loose in the garden will want to run and explore, and he should be granted that freedom. Do not let a fence give you a false sense of security; you would be surprised how crafty (and persistent) a dog can be in figuring out how to dig under and squeeze his way through small holes, or to jump or climb over a fence. The remedy is to make the fence high enough so that it really is impossible for

'You can't teach an old dog new tricks' is an untrue expression, but it is easier to train a pup.

your dog to get over it (about 3 metres should suffice), and well embedded into the ground. Be sure to repair or secure any gaps in the fence. Check the fence periodically to ensure that it is in good shape and make repairs as needed; a very determined pup may return to the same spot to 'work on it' until he is able to get through.

FIRST TRIP TO THE VET
You have picked out your puppy, and your home and family are ready. Now all you have to do is collect your Golden Retriever from the breeder and the fun begins, right? Well...not so fast. Something else you need to prepare is your pup's first trip to the veterinary surgeon. Perhaps the breeder can recommend someone in the area that specialises in Golden Retrievers, or maybe you know some other Golden Retriever owners who can

Keep your eye on your dog when your flowers bloom. The scent brings both retrievers (they have very sensitive noses) and biting insects together. Blooming flowers should be off-limits to your Golden. Goldens are frequently allergic to flower pollen.

suggest a good vet. Either way, you should have an appointment arranged for your pup before you pick him up and plan on taking him for an examination before bringing him home.

The pup's first visit will consist of an overall examination to make sure that the pup does not have any problems that are not apparent to the eye. The veterinary surgeon will also set up a schedule for the pup's vaccinations; the breeder will inform you of which ones the pup has already received and the vet can continue from there.

INTRODUCTION TO THE FAMILY
Everyone in the house will be excited about the puppy

coming home and will want to pet him and play with him, but it is best to make the introduction low-key so as not to overwhelm the puppy. He is apprehensive already. It is the first time he has been separated from his mother and the breeder, and the ride to your

If you own a Golden Retriever, you must have a trusted vet to maintain your dog in good health, to arrange a vaccination schedule and to recommend the most up-to-date medications as needed.

DID YOU KNOW?

The electrical fencing system which forms an invisible fence works on a battery-operated collar that shocks the dog if it gets too close to the buried (or elevated) wire. There are some people who think very highly of this system of controlling a dog's wandering. Keep in mind that the collar has batteries. For safety's sake, replace the batteries every month with the best quality batteries available.

The pup may approach the family members or may busy himself with exploring for a while. Gradually, each person should spend some time with the pup, one at a time, crouching down to get as close to the pup's level as possible and letting him sniff their hands and petting him gently. He

home is likely the first time he has been in an auto. The last thing you want to do is smother him, as this will only frighten him further. This is not to say that human contact is not extremely necessary at this stage, because this is the time when a connection between the pup and his human family is formed. Gentle petting and soothing words should help console him, as well as just putting him down and letting him explore on his own (under your watchful eye, of course).

DID YOU KNOW?

Grooming tools, collars, leashes, dog beds and, of course, toys will be an expense to you when you first obtain your pup, and the cost will trickle on throughout your dog's lifetime. If your puppy damages or destroys your possessions (as most puppies surely will!) or something belonging to a neighbour, you can calculate additional expense. There is also flea and pest control, which every dog owner faces more than once. You must be able to handle the financial responsibility of owning a dog.

49

definitely needs human attention and he needs to be touched—this is how to form an immediate bond. Just remember that the pup is experiencing a lot of things for the first time, at the same time. There are new people, new noises, new smells, and new things to investigate: so be gentle, be affectionate, and be as comforting as you can be.

Even a frightened Golden Retriever will welcome attention from his new family members. Most Golden pups adjust quite easily to their new environment.

DID YOU KNOW?
Training your puppy takes much patience and can be frustrating at times, but you should see results from your efforts. If you have a puppy that seems untrainable, take him to a trainer or behaviourist. The dog may have a personality problem that requires the help of a professional, or perhaps you need help in learning how to train your dog.

YOUR PUP'S FIRST NIGHT HOME

You have travelled home with your new charge safely in his basket or crate. He has been to the vet for a thorough check-over; he has been weighed, his papers examined; perhaps he has even been vaccinated and wormed as well. He has met the family, licked the whole family, including the excited children and the less-than-happy cat. He has explored his area, his new bed, the garden and anywhere else he has been permitted. He has eaten his first meal at home and relieved himself in the proper place. He has heard lots of new sounds, smelled new friends and seen more of the outside world than ever before.

That was just the first day! He has tuckered out and is ready for bed...or so you think!

It is puppy's first night and you are ready to say 'Good

PHOTO COURTESY OF GOLD-RUSH KENNELS

process throughout throughout the night. Beyond that, if the puppy needs to relieve himself during the night, you will be able to whisk him out immediately. Do not ever give in and remove him from his crate or allow him into bed with you.

Breeders arrange for their puppies to meet new people whilst still with their dam. These pups are always the best socialised.

night'—keep in mind that this is puppy's first night ever to be sleeping alone. His dam and littermates are no longer at paw's length and he is a bit scared, cold and lonely. Be reassuring to your new family member. This is not the time to spoil him and give in to his inevitable whining.

Puppies whine. They whine to let the others know where they are and hopefully to get company out of it. Place your pup in his new bed or crate in his room and close the door. Mercifully, he may fall asleep without a peep. If the inevitable occurs, ignore the whining: he is fine. Be strong and keep his interest in mind. Do not allow your heart to become guilty and visit the pup. He will fall asleep.

Some breeders suggest moving the crate into your bedroom at night for the first several weeks. Sleeping in your room will not spoil the puppy. It will make him feel secure and continue the bonding

DID YOU KNOW?

Chewing goes hand in hand with nipping in the sense that a teething puppy is always looking for a way to soothe his aching gums. In this case, instead of chewing on you, he may have taken a liking to your favourite shoe or something else which he should not be chewing. Again, realise that this is a normal canine behaviour that does not need to be discouraged, only redirected. Your pup just needs to be taught what is acceptable to chew on and what is off limits. Consistently tell him NO when you catch him chewing on something forbidden and give him a chew toy. Conversely, praise him when you catch him chewing on something appropriate. In this way you are discouraging the inappropriate behaviour and reinforcing the desired behaviour. The puppy chewing should stop after his adult teeth have come in, but an adult dog continues to chew for various reasons—perhaps because he is bored, perhaps to relieve tension, or perhaps he just likes to chew. That is why it is important to redirect his chewing when he is still young.

What could be as reliable and consistent as the mail carrier? Here's a Golden exception to the rule.

Many breeders recommend placing a piece of bedding from his former homestead in his new bed so that he recognises the scent of his littermates. Others still advise placing a hot water bottle in his bed for warmth. This latter may be a good idea provided the pup does not attempt to suckle—he will get good and wet and may not fall asleep so fast.

Puppy's first night can be somewhat stressful for the pup and his new family. Remember that you are setting the tone of nighttime at your house. Unless you want to play with your pup every evening at 10 p.m., midnight and 2 a.m., do not initiate the habit. Your family will thank you, and so will your pup!

DID YOU KNOW?

Taking your dog from the breeder to your home in a car can be a very uncomfortable experience for both of you. The puppy will have been taken from his warm, friendly, safe environment and brought into a strange new environment. An environment that moves! Be prepared for loose bowels, urination, crying, whining and even fear biting. With proper love and encouragement when you arrive home, the stress of the trip should quickly disappear.

PREVENTING PUPPY PROBLEMS
SOCIALISATION

Now that you have done all of the preparatory work and have helped your pup get accustomed to his new home and family, it is about time for you to have some fun! Socialising your Golden Retriever pup gives you the opportunity to show off your new friend, and your pup gets to reap the benefits of being an adorable furry creature that people will coo over, want to pet and, in general, think is absolutely precious!

Besides getting to know his new family, your puppy should be exposed to other people, animals and situations. This will help him become well adjusted as he grows up and less prone to being timid or fearful of the new things he will encounter. Your pup's socialisation began at the breeder's but now it is your responsibility to continue it. The socialisation he receives up until the age of 16 to 20 weeks is the most critical, as this is the time when he forms his impressions of the outside world. Be especially careful during the eight-to-ten-week period, also known as the fear period. The interaction he receives during this time should be gentle and reassuring. Lack of socialisation can manifest itself in fear and aggression as the dog grows up. He needs lots of human contact, affection, handling and exposure to other animals.

Once your pup has received his necessary vaccinations, feel free to take him out and about (on his lead, of course). Walk him around the neighbourhood, take him on your daily errands, let people pet him, let him meet other dogs and pets, etc.

DID YOU KNOW?
Thorough socialisation includes not only meeting new people but also being introduced to new experiences such as riding in the auto, having his coat brushed, hearing the television, walking in a crowd—the list is endless. The more your pup experiences, and the more positive the experiences are, the less of a shock and the less scary it will be for your pup to encounter new things.

Puppies do not have to try to make friends; there will be no shortage of people who will want to introduce themselves. Just make sure that you carefully supervise each meeting. If the neighbourhood children want to say hello, for example, that is great—children and pups most often make great companions. Sometimes an excited child can unintentionally handle a pup too roughly, or an overzealous pup can playfully nip a little too hard. You want to make socialisation experiences positive ones. What a pup learns during this very formative stage will impact his attitude toward future encounters. You want your dog to be comfortable around everyone. A pup that has a bad experience with a child may grow up to be a dog that is shy around or aggressive toward children.

Puppies should be accustomed to relieving themselves outdoors in designated areas. This is called *housebreaking*.

53

Golden puppies are very dependent creatures. In your new home, they will rely on you for food, water, shelter, leadership and companionship.

CONSISTENCY IN TRAINING

Dogs, being pack animals, naturally need a leader, or else they try to establish dominance in their packs. When you bring a dog into your family, the choice of who becomes the leader and who becomes the 'pack' is entirely up to you! Your pup's intuitive quest for dominance, coupled with the fact that it is nearly impossible to look at an adorable Golden Retriever pup, with his 'puppy-dog' eyes and his too-big-for his-head-still-floppy ears, and not cave in, give the pup almost an unfair advantage in getting the upper hand! A pup will definitely test

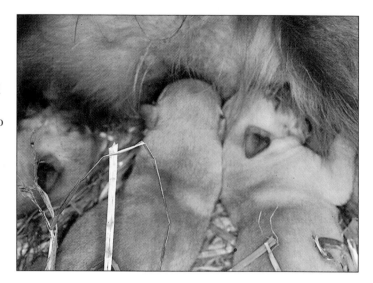

You can lead a Golden pup to water, but you can't keep him from playing.

the waters to see what he can and cannot do. Do not give in to those pleading eyes—stand your ground when it comes to disciplining the pup and make sure that all family members do the same. It will only confuse the pup when Mother tells him to get off the couch when he is used to sitting up there with Father to watch the nightly news. Avoid discrepancies by having all members of the household decide on the rules before the pup even comes home…and be consistent in enforcing them! Early training shapes the dog's personality, so you cannot be unclear in what you expect.

You may want to attend a puppy class and early obedience training with your puppy. A class environment is good social stimulation for the puppy and for you. It will also motivate you to train your puppy and practise when you are not in class so you do not appear foolish in front of your trainer and fellow puppy owners. Investigate the cost of puppy lessons so you do not omit this important aspect of Golden ownership.

COMMON PUPPY PROBLEMS

The best way to prevent puppy problems is to be proactive in stopping an undesirable behaviour as soon as it starts. The old saying 'You can't teach an old dog new tricks' does not necessarily hold true, but it is true that it is much easier to discourage bad behaviour in a young developing pup than to wait until the pup's bad behaviour becomes the adult dog's bad habit. There are some problems that are especially prevalent in puppies as they develop.

NIPPING

As puppies start to teethe, they feel the need to sink their teeth into anything available...unfortunately that includes your fingers, arms, hair, and toes. You may find this behaviour cute for the

The toughest night with your Golden puppy will be the first night, for both the puppy and the family.

first five seconds...until you feel just how sharp those puppy teeth are. This is something you want to discourage immediately and consistently with a firm 'No!' (or whatever number of firm 'No's' it takes for him to understand that you mean business). Then replace your finger with an appropriate chow

Puppies enjoy all kinds of toys, especially stuffed animals that squeak. Do not allow children to provoke the puppy as this can lead to nipping.

toy. Whilst this behaviour is merely annoying when the dog is young, it can become dangerous as your Golden Retriever's adult teeth grow in and his jaws develop, and he continues to think it is okay to gnaw on human appendages. This is a very oral breed with a natural tendency to chew and nip. He does not mean any harm with a friendly nip, but he also does not know his own strength.

CRYING/WHINING

Your pup will often cry, whine, whimper, howl or make some type of commotion when he is left alone. This is basically his way of calling out for attention to make sure that you know he is there and that you have not forgotten about him. He feels insecure when he is left alone, when you are out of the house and he is in his crate or when you are in another part of the house and he cannot see you. The noise he is making is an expression of the anxiety he feels at being alone, so he needs to be taught that being alone is okay. You are not actually training the dog to stop making noise, you are training him to feel comfortable when he is alone and thus removing the need for him to make the noise. This is where the crate filled with cosy blankets and toys comes in handy. You want to know that he is safe when you are

not there to supervise, and you know that he will be safe in his crate rather than roaming freely about the house. In order for the pup to stay in his crate without making a fuss, he needs to be comfortable in his crate. On that note, it is extremely important that the crate is never used as a form of punishment, or the pup will have a negative association with the crate.

Accustom the pup to the crate in short, gradually increasing time intervals in which you put him in the crate, maybe with a treat, and stay in the room with him. If he cries or makes a fuss, do not go to him, but stay in his sight. Gradually he will realise that staying in his crate is all right without your help, and it will not be so traumatic for him when you are not around. You may want to leave the radio on softly when you leave the house; the sound of human voices may be comforting to him.

> **DID YOU KNOW?**
> Scour your carport for potential puppy dangers. Remove weed killers, pesticides and antifreeze materials. Antifreeze is highly toxic and even a few drops can kill an adult dog. The sweet taste attracts the animal, who will quickly consume it from the floor or curbside.

POISONOUS PLANTS

Below is a partial list of plants that are considered poisonous. These plants can cause skin irritation, illness and even death. You should be aware of the types of plants that grow in your garden and that you keep in your home. Special care should be taken to rid your garden of dangerous plants and to keep all plants in the household out of your Golden Retriever's reach.

American Blue Flag
Bachelor's Button
Barberry
Bog Iris
Boxwood
Buttercup
Cherry Pits
Chinese Arbor
Chokecherry
Christmas Rose
Climbing Lily
Crown of Thorns
Elderberry (berries)
Elephant Ear
English Ivy
False Acacia
Fern
Foxglove
Hellebore
Herb of Grace
Holly
Horse Chestnut
Iris (bulb)

Japanese Yew
Jerusalem Cherry
Jimson Weed
Lenten Rose
Lily of the Valley
Marigold
Milkwort
Mistletoe (berries)
Monkshood
Mullein
Narcissus
Peony
Persian Ivy
Rhododendron
Rhubarb
Shallon
Siberian Iris
Solomon's Seal
Star of Bethlehem
Water Lily
Wood Spurge
Wisteria
Yew

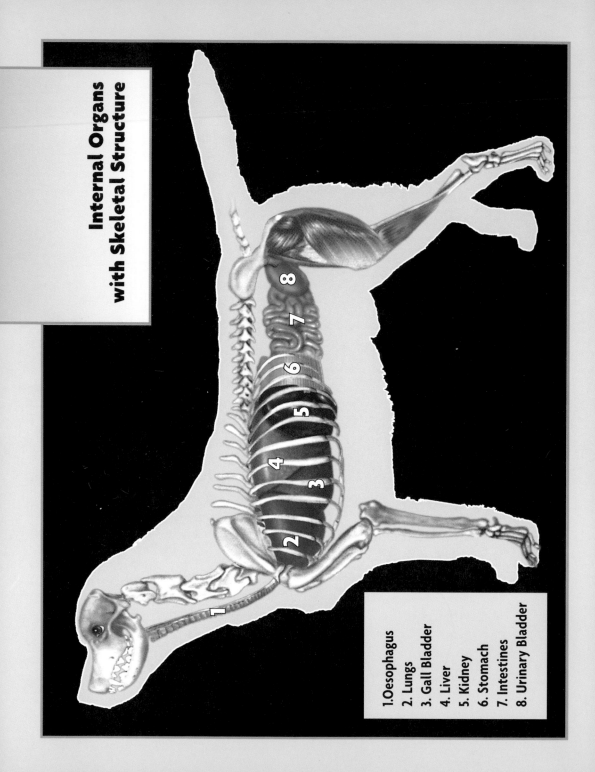

Internal Organs with Skeletal Structure

1. Oesophagus
2. Lungs
3. Gall Bladder
4. Liver
5. Kidney
6. Stomach
7. Intestines
8. Urinary Bladder

EVERYDAY CARE OF YOUR
Golden Retriever

DIETARY AND FEEDING CONSIDERATIONS

You have probably heard it a thousand times, 'you are what you eat.' Believe it or not, it's very true. Dogs are what you feed them because they have little choice in the matter. Even those people who truly want to feed their dogs the best often cannot do so because they do not know which foods are best for their dog.

Dog foods are produced in three basic types: dried, semi-moist and tinned. Dried foods are the choice of the cost conscious because they are much less expensive than semi-moist and canned. Dried foods contain the least fat and the most preservatives. Most tinned foods are 60–70-percent water, whilst semi-moist foods are so full of sugar that they are the least preferred by owners, though dogs welcome them (as a child does sweets). You must always feed your Golden a quality food, and such a product will cost more than generic and over-the-counter brands sold at a local grocery store.

Three stages of development must be considered when selecting a diet for your dog: the puppy stage, the mid-age or adult stage and the senior age or geriatric stage.

PUPPY STAGE

Puppies have a natural instinct to suck milk from their mother's teats. They

Golden Retrievers simply must be fed a proper, balanced diet in order to stay healthy and fit. Read the labels and compare the contents and prices.

Your Golden Retriever breeder will advise you on the best brand food to feed your puppy. It is recommended to continue feeding the same brand that the breeder has been offering.

exhibit this behaviour from the first moments of their lives. If they don't suckle within a short while, the breeder attempts to put them onto their mother's nipple. A newborn's failure to suckle often requires that the breeder handfeed the pup under the guidance of a veterinary surgeon. This involves a baby bottle and a special formula. Their mother's milk is much better than any formula because it contains colostrum, a sort of antibiotic milk that protects the puppy during the first eight to ten weeks of their lives.

Puppies should be allowed to nurse for six weeks and they should be slowly weaned away from their mother by introducing small portions of tinned meat after they are about one

DID YOU KNOW?

Selecting the best dry dog food is difficult. There is no majority consensus among veterinary scientists as to the value of nutrient analyses (protein, fat, fibre, moisture, ash, cholesterol, minerals, etc.). All agree that feeding trials are what matters, but you also have to consider the individual dog. Its weight, age, activity and what pleases its taste, all must be considered. It is probably best to take the advice of your veterinary surgeon. Every dog's dietary requirements vary, even during the lifetime of a particular dog.

If your dog is fed a good dry food, it does not require supplements of meat or vegetables. Dogs do appreciate a little variety in their diets so you may choose to stay with the same brand, but vary the flavour. Alternatively you may wish to add a little flavoured stock to give a difference to the taste.

DID YOU KNOW?

You must store your dried dog food carefully. Open packages of dog food quickly lose their vitamin value, usually within 90 days of being opened. Mould spores and vermin could also contaminate the food.

month old. Then dry food is gradually added to the puppies' portions over the next few weeks.

By the time they are eight weeks old, they should be completely weaned and fed solely a puppy dried food. During this weaning period, their diet is most important as the puppy grows fastest during its first year of life.

Golden Retriever pups should be fed three meals per day when they are six to eight weeks of age. At eight weeks, the pup can be fed twice per day. Fussy eaters may require an additional smaller meal to maintain a good weight. Growth foods can be recommended by your veterinary surgeon and the puppy should be kept on this diet for up to 12 months.

Puppy diets should be balanced for your dog's needs, and supplements of vitamins, minerals and protein should not be necessary.

ADULT DIETS

A dog is considered an adult when it has stopped growing in height and/or length. Do not consider the dog's weight when the decision is made to switch from a puppy diet to a maintenance diet. Again

Golden Retriever puppies should be allowed to nurse for at least six weeks before they begin to be weaned. The last two weeks of this period should begin the slow introduction of tinned meat.

Once a puppy is in your home, it may not eat as vigorously as it did while at the breeder's home. Competition for food at the feed tray incites the puppies' appetites.

Do You Know What You Are Feeding Your Dog?

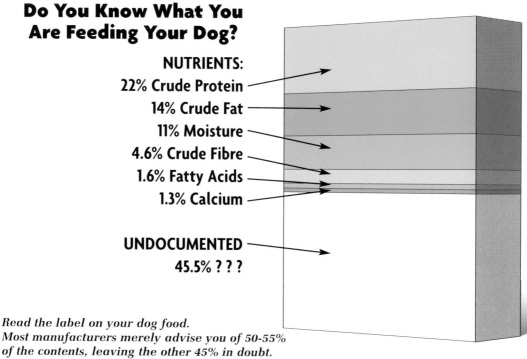

NUTRIENTS:

22% Crude Protein

14% Crude Fat

11% Moisture

4.6% Crude Fibre

1.6% Fatty Acids

1.3% Calcium

UNDOCUMENTED

45.5% ? ? ?

Read the label on your dog food.
Most manufacturers merely advise you of 50-55%
of the contents, leaving the other 45% in doubt.

DID YOU KNOW?

The cost of food must also be mentioned. All dogs need a good quality food with an adequate supply of protein to develop their bones and muscles properly. Most dogs are not picky eaters but unless fed properly they can quickly succumb to skin problems.

you should rely upon your veterinary surgeon to recommend an acceptable maintenance diet. Major dog food manufacturers specialise in this type of food and it is just necessary for you to select the one best suited to your dog's needs. Active dogs may have different requirements than sedate dogs.

A Golden Retriever is fully mature around 12 months of age, though it often takes another 12 to 18 months for dog to reach its peak as a performance animal.

SENIOR DIETS

As dogs get older, their metabolism changes. The older dog usually exercises less, moves more slowly and sleeps more. This change in lifestyle and physiological performance requires a change in diet. Since these changes take

place slowly, they might not be recognisable. What is easily recognisable is weight gain. By continually feeding your dog an adult maintenance diet when it is

Your Golden is not considered an adult until he stops growing.

slowing down metabolically, your dog will gain weight. Obesity in an older dog compounds the health problems that already accompany old age.

As your dog gets older, few of their organs function up to par. The kidneys slow down and the intestines

DID YOU KNOW?

Many adult diets are based on grain. There is nothing wrong with this as long as it does not contain soy meal. Diets based on soy often cause flatulence (passing gas).

Grain-based diets are almost always the least expensive and a good grain diet is just as good as the most expensive diet containing animal protein.

There are many cases, however, when your dog might require a special diet. These special requirements should only be recommended by your veterinary surgeon.

Whilst many dogs do well on light or senior diets, other dogs do better on puppy diets or other special premium diets such as lamb and rice.

Be sensitive to your senior Golden Retriever's diet and this will help control other problems that may arise with your old friend.

As your Golden Retriever matures, his dietary needs change. Active working dogs will require a different nutritional base than will ordinary house dogs.

become less efficient. These age-related factors are best handled with a change in diet and a change in feeding schedule to give smaller portions that are more easily digested.

There is no single best diet for every older dog.

WATER
Just as your dog needs proper nutrition from his food, water is an essential "nutrient" as well. Water keeps the dog's body properly hydrated and promotes normal function of the body's systems. During housebreak-

Since the Golden Retriever was developed as a water dog, puppies have an incurable affinity to water.

ing it is necessary to keep an eye on how much water your Golden Retriever is drinking, but once he is reliably trained he should have access to clean fresh water at all times. Make sure that the dog's water bowl is clean, and change the water often.

Clean water should be available to all dogs. Golden Retriever puppies would rather swim in water than drink it.

EXERCISE

All dogs require some form of exercise, regardless of breed. A sedentary lifestyle is as harmful to a dog as it is to a person. The Golden Retriever is a sporting dog with an abundance of energy and enthusiasm. Regular walks, play sessions in the garden, or letting the dog run free in the garden under your supervision are all sufficient forms of exercise for the Golden Retriever. For those who are more ambitious, you will find that your Golden Retriever will be able to keep up with you on extra long walks or the morning run. Not only is exercise essential

Exercise is required for your Golden Retriever's mental and physical well being. It's great for the owner's good health too.

> ### DID YOU KNOW?
>
> Dog food must be at room temperature, neither too hot nor too cold. Fresh water, changed daily and served in a clean bowl, is mandatory, especially when feeding dry food.
>
> Never feed your dog from the table while you are eating. Never feed your dog left-overs from your own meal. They usually contain too much fat and too much seasoning.
>
> Dogs must chew their food. Hard pellets are excellent; soups and slurries are to be avoided.
>
> Don't add left-overs or any extras to normal dog food. The normal food is usually balanced and adding something extra destroys the balance.
>
> Except for age-related changes, dogs do not require dietary variations. They can be fed the same diet, day after day, without their becoming bored or ill.

PHOTO BY KENT AND DONNA DANNEN

If you play ball with a Golden Retriever, be sure the ball is large and tough enough that your dog cannot destroy or swallow it.

to keep the dog's body fit, it is essential to his mental well being. A bored dog will find something to do, which often manifests itself in some type of destructive behaviour. In this sense, it is essential for the owner's mental well being as well!

GROOMING
BRUSHING
The luxurious Golden coat is both a bane and a blessing. Lovely to look at, yes, but frequent grooming is required to keep it healthy and attractive. Twice-weekly brushing sessions are a must if you hope to control casting coat and keep those silky strands from floating onto

your furniture and into your salad bowl. Casting coat is most troublesome in spring and again in fall when the Golden casts its downy undercoat to prepare for the changing season. That often surprises a new owner who is not prepared for clouds of dog down rolling across the floors and carpets.

BATHING
Dogs do not need to be bathed as often as humans, but regular bathing is essential for healthy skin and a healthy, shiny coat. Again, like most anything, if you accustom your pup to being bathed as a puppy, it will be

DID YOU KNOW?
How much grooming equipment you purchase will depend on how much grooming you are going to do. Here are some basics:

• Natural bristle brush
• Slicker brush
• Metal comb
• Scissors
• Blaster
• Rubber mat
• Dog shampoo
• Spray hose attachment
• Ear cleaner
• Cotton wipes
• Towels
• Nail clippers

should purchase a shampoo that is made for dogs. Do not use a product made for human hair. Wash the head last; you do not want shampoo to drip into the dog's eyes whilst you are washing the rest of his body. Work the shampoo all the way down to the skin. You can use this opportunity to check the skin for any bumps, bites or other abnormalities. Do not neglect any area of the body—get all of the hard-to-reach places.

Once the dog has been thoroughly shampooed, he requires an equally thorough rinsing. Shampoo left in the coat can be irritating to the skin. Protect his eyes from the shampoo by shielding

Before bathing your Golden Retriever, use a natural bristle brush to reach through the top coat.

second nature by the time he grows up. You want your dog to be at ease in the bath or else it could end up a wet, soapy, messy ordeal for both of you!

Brush your Golden Retriever thoroughly before wetting his coat. This will get rid of most matts and tangles, which are harder to remove when the coat is wet. Make sure that your dog has a good non-slip surface to stand on. Begin by wetting the dog's coat. A shower or hose attachment is necessary for thoroughly wetting and rinsing the coat. Check the water temperature to make sure that it is neither too hot nor too cold.

Next, apply shampoo to the dog's coat and work it into a good lather. You

A Golden should be groomed daily, but a minimum schedule is twice a week of intense brushing and combing. Use a metal comb to untangle knots.

them with your hand and directing the flow of water in the opposite direction. You should also avoid getting water in the ear canal. Be prepared for your dog to shake out his coat—you might want to stand back, but make sure you have a hold on the dog to keep him from running through the house.

Grooming your Golden should be a pleasure, not a chore.

EAR CLEANING
The ears should be kept clean and any excess hair inside the ear should be trimmed. Ears can be cleaned with cotton wipes and special cleaner or ear powder made especially for dogs. Be on the lookout for any signs of infection or ear mite

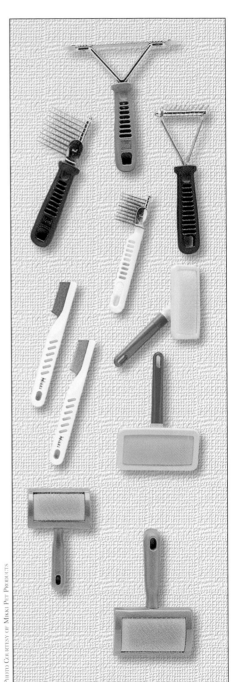

Since Goldens love the water, they are easily bathed in a small pool outdoors when the weather permits.

PHOTO COURTESY OF MIKKI PET PRODUCTS.

infestation. If your Golden Retriever has been shaking his head or scratching at his ears frequently, this usually indicates a problem. If his ears have an unusual odour, this is a sure sign of mite infestation or infection, and a signal to have his ears checked by the veterinary surgeon.

NAIL CLIPPING
Your Golden Retriever should be accustomed to having his nails trimmed at an

early age, since it will be part of your maintenance routine throughout his life. Not only does it look nicer, but a dog with long nails can cause injury if he jumps up or if he scratches someone unintentionally. Also, a long nail has a better chance of ripping and bleeding, or causing the feet to spread. A good rule of thumb is that if you can hear your dog's nails clicking on the floor when he walks, his nails are too long.

Before you start cutting, make sure you can identify the 'quick' in each nail. The quick is a blood vessel that runs through the

If you have a swimming pool, you will have to train your Golden how to enter and exit properly. Goldens love to take a dip on their own, but you must keep a close eye on them.

THE WASH CYCLE...
The use of human soap products like shampoo, bubble bath and hand soap can be damaging to a dog's coat and skin. Human products are too strong and remove the protective oils coating the dog's hair and skin (making him water-resistant). Use only shampoo made especially for dogs and you may like to use a medicated shampoo which will always help to keep external parasites at bay.

THE DRY CYCLE...
Once you are sure that the dog is thoroughly rinsed, squeeze the excess water out of the coat with your hand and dry him with a heavy towel. You may choose to use a blaster on his coat or just let it dry naturally. In cold weather, never allow your dog outside with a wet coat.

There are 'dry bath' products on the market, which are sprays and powders intended for spot cleaning, that can be used between regular baths, if necessary. They are not substitutes for regular baths, but they are easy to use for touch-ups as they do not require rinsing.

Introduce the puppy to the bath at a young age. Compared to most other breeds, Goldens are amongst the easiest dogs to accustom to the bathing routine.

69

centre of each nail and grows rather close to the end. It will bleed if accidentally cut, which will be quite painful for the dog as it contains nerve endings. Keep some type of clotting agent on hand, such as a styptic pencil or styptic powder (the type used for shaving). This will stop the bleeding quickly when applied to the end of the cut nail. Do not panic if this happens, just stop the bleeding and talk soothingly to your dog. Once he has calmed down, move on to the next nail. It is better to clip a little at a time, particularly with black-nailed dogs.

Hold your pup steady as you begin trimming his nails; you do not want him to make any sudden movements or run away. Talk to him soothingly and stroke his fur as you clip. Holding his foot in your

You should trim your Golden's nails carefully so that you don't cut the quick. Clip a little at a time to avoid the possibility of hurting the dog, especially in dark nails where the quick is hard to see.

DID YOU KNOW?

A dog that spends a lot of time outside on a hard surface such as cement or pavement will have his nails naturally worn down and may not need to have them trimmed as often, except maybe in the colder months when he is not outside as much. Regardless, it is best to get your dog accustomed to this procedure at an early age so that he is used to it. Some dogs are especially sensitive about having their feet touched, but if a dog has experienced it since he was young, he should not be bothered by it.

Your Golden puppy's ears should be cleaned weekly with a cotton wool bud or specially made wipes for ear cleaning.

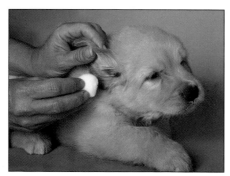

hand, simply take off the end of each nail in one quick clip. You can purchase nail clippers that are specially made for dogs; you can probably find them wherever you buy pet or grooming supplies.

TRAVELLING WITH YOUR DOG
AUTOMOBILE TRAVEL
You should accustom your Golden Retriever to riding in a car at an early age. You may or may not take him in the car often, but at the very least he will need to go to the vet and you do not want these trips to be traumatic for the dog or a big hassle for you. The safest way for a dog to ride

in the car is in his crate. If he uses a fibreglass crate in the house, you can use the same crate for travel. Wire crates can be used for travel, but fibreglass or wooden crates are safer.

Put the pup in the crate and see how he reacts. If he seems uneasy, you can have a passenger hold him on his lap whilst you drive. Another option is a specially made safety harness for dogs, which straps the dog in much like a seat belt. Do not let the dog roam loose in the vehicle— this is very dangerous! If you should stop short, your dog can be thrown and injured. If the dog starts climbing on you and pestering you whilst you are driving, you will not

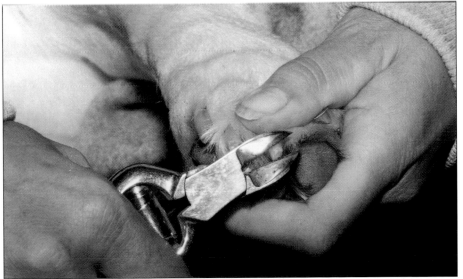

There are many types of nail clippers available at your local pet shop for clipping the Golden's nails.

Your Golden should never be loose in the car when you are driving. For long-distance trips, a large crate in the back of the vehicle is the safest option.

be able to concentrate on the road. It is an unsafe situation for everyone—human and canine.

For long trips, be prepared to stop to let the dog relieve himself. Bring along whatever you need to clean up after him. You should bring along some old towels and rags, should he have an accident in the car or become carsick.

AIR TRAVEL

If bringing your dog on a flight, you will have to contact the airline to make special arrangements. It is rather common for dogs to travel by air, but advance permission is usually required. The dog will be required to travel in a fibreglass crate; you may be able to use your own or the airline can usually supply one. To help the dog be at ease, put one of his favourite toys in the crate with him. Do not feed the dog for at least six hours before the trip to minimise his need to relieve himself. However, certain regulations specify that water must always be made available to the dog in the crate.

Make sure your dog is properly identified and that your contact information appears on his ID tags and on his crate. Animals travel in a different area of the plane than human passengers, and,

DID YOU KNOW?

When travelling, never let your dog off-lead in a strange area. Your dog could run away out of fear or decide to

chase a passing chipmunk or cat or simply want to stretch his legs without restriction—you might never see your canine friend again.

although transporting animals is routine for large airlines, there is always the slight risk of getting separated from your dog.

BOARDING

So you want to take a family holiday—and you want to include all members of the family. You would probably make arrangements for accommodations ahead of time anyway, but this is especially important when travelling with a dog. You do not want to make an overnight stop at the only place around for miles and find out that they do not

allow dogs. Also, you do not want to reserve a place for your family without confirming that you are travelling with a dog because if it is against their policy you may not have a place to stay.

Alternatively, if you are travelling and choose not to bring your Golden Retriever, you will have to make arrangements for him whilst you are away. Some options are to bring him to a neighbour's house to stay whilst you are gone, to have a trusted neighbour stop by often or stay at your house, or bring your dog to a reputable boarding kennel. If you choose to board him at a kennel, you should stop by to see the facility and where the dogs are kept to make

DID YOU KNOW?

For international travel you will have to make arrangements well in advance (perhaps months), as countries' regulations pertaining to bringing in animals differ. There may be special health certificates and/or vaccinations that your dog will need before taking the trip, sometimes this has to be done within a certain time frame. In rabies-free countries, you will need to bring proof of the dog's rabies vaccination and there may be a quarantine period upon arrival.

If you cannot take your dog with you on holiday, you should locate a suitable kennel in your area to ensure that your dog is in good hands whilst you travel.

DID YOU KNOW?

If your dog gets lost, he is not able to ask for directions home.

Identification tags fastened to the collar give important information—the dog's name, the owner's name, the owner's address and a telephone number where the owner can be reached. This makes it easy for whoever finds the dog to contact the owner and arrange to have the dog returned. An added advantage is that a person will be more likely to approach a lost dog who has ID tags on his collar; it tells the person that this is somebody's pet rather than a stray. This is the easiest and fastest method of identification provided that the tags stay on the collar and the collar stays on the dog.

sure that it is clean. Talk to some of the employees and see how they treat the dogs—do they spend time with the dogs, play with them, exercise them, etc.? You know that your Golden Retriever will not be happy unless he gets regular activity. Also find out the kennel's policy on vaccinations and what they require. This is for all of the dogs' safety, since when dogs are kept together, there is a greater risk of diseases being passed from dog to dog. Many veterinary surgeons offer boarding facilities; this is another option.

IDENTIFICATION

Your Golden Retriever is your valued companion and friend. That is why you always keep a close eye on him and you have made sure that he cannot escape from the garden or wriggle out of his collar and run away from you. However, accidents can happen and there may come a time when your dog unexpectedly gets

separated from you. If this unfortunate event should occur, the first thing on your mind will be finding him. Proper identification, including an ID tag, a tattoo, and possibly a microchip, will increase the chances of his being returned to you safely and quickly.

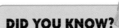

DID YOU KNOW?

As puppies become more and more expensive, especially those puppies of high quality for showing and/or breeding, they have a greater chance of being stolen. The usual collar dog tag is, of course, easily removed. But there are two techniques that have become widely utilised for identification.

The puppy microchip implantation involves the injection of a small microchip, about the size of a corn kernel, under the skin of the dog. If your dog shows up at a clinic or shelter, or is offered for resale under less than savory circumstances, it can be positively identified by the microchip. The microchip is scanned and a registry quickly identifies you as the owner. This is not only protection against theft, but should the dog run away or go chasing a squirrel and get lost, you have a fair chance of getting it back.

Tattooing is done on various parts of the dog, from its belly to its cheeks. The number tattooed can be your telephone number or any other number which you can easily memorise. When professional dog thieves see a tattooed dog, they usually lose interest in it. Both microchipping and tattooing can be done at your local veterinary clinic. For the safety of our dogs, no laboratory facility or dog broker will accept a tattooed dog as stock.

DID YOU KNOW?

You have a valuable dog. If the dog is lost or stolen you would undoubtedly become extremely upset. If you encounter a lost dog, notify the police or the local animal shelter.

Be certain that your Golden's collar fits properly and that its identification tags are attached securely.

Golden Retrievers love the water and are not afraid to jump, even from heights. Hunting dogs develop true style and talent in their 'diving' patterns.

Your Golden
Retriever puppy is
an open canvas.
Everything he
becomes is
dependent on the
education, patience
and energy of
his owner.

HOUSEBREAKING AND TRAINING YOUR
Golden Retriever

Living with an untrained dog is a lot like owning a piano that you do not know how to play—it is a nice object to look at but it does not do much more than that to bring you pleasure. Now try taking piano lessons and suddenly the piano comes alive and brings forth magical sounds and rhythms that set your heart singing and your body swaying.

The same is true with your Golden Retriever. At first you enjoy seeing him around the house. He does not do much with you other than to need food, water and exercise. Come to think of it, he does not bring you much joy, either. He is a big responsibility with a very small return. Often he develops unacceptable behaviours that annoy and/or infuriate you to say nothing of bad habits that may end up costing you great sums of money. Not a good thing!

Now train your Golden Retriever. Enrol in an obedience class. Teach him good manners as you learn how and why he behaves the way he does. Find out how to communicate with your dog and how to recognise and understand his communica-

tions with you. Suddenly the dog takes on a new role in your life— he is smart, interesting, well behaved and fun to be with. He demonstrates his bond of devotion to you daily. In other words, your Golden Retriever does wonders for your ego because he constantly reminds you that you are not only his leader, you are his hero! Miraculous things have

You are personally and solely responsible for moulding and training your Golden Retriever puppy. Are you ready for this responsibility?

happened—you have a wonderful dog (even your family and friends have noticed the transformation!) and you feel good about yourself.

Those involved with teaching dog obedience and counselling owners about their dogs' behaviour have discovered some interesting facts about dog ownership. For

Training the Golden puppy should involve the whole family. Every member of the family must understand what is expected of the puppy and how to instruct it.

example, training dogs when they are puppies results in the highest rate of success in developing well-mannered and well-adjusted adult dogs. Training an older dog, from six months to six years of age, can produce almost equal results providing that the owner accepts the dog's slower rate of learning capability and is willing to work patiently to

help the dog succeed at developing to his fullest potential. Unfortunately, many owners of untrained adult dogs lack the patience factor, so they do not persist until their dogs are successful at learning particular behaviours.

Training a puppy, aged 8 to 16 weeks (20 weeks at the most) is like working with a dry sponge in a pool of water. The pup soaks up whatever you show him and constantly looks for more things to do and learn. At this early age, his body is not yet producing hormones, and therein lies the reason for such a high rate of success. Without hormones, he is focused on his owners and not particularly interested in investigating other places, dogs, people, etc. You are his leader: his provider of food, water, shelter and security. He latches onto you and wants to stay close. He will usually follow you from room to room, will not let you out of his sight when you are outdoors with him, and respond in like

DID YOU KNOW?

Taking your dog to an obedience school may be the best investment in time and money you can ever make. You will enjoy the benefits for the lifetime of your dog and you will have the opportunity to meet people with your similar expectations for companion dogs.

manner to the people and animals you encounter. If you greet a friend warmly, he will be happy to greet the person as well. If, however, you are

untrained dog begins to wander away from you and even ignore your commands to stay close. When this behaviour becomes a problem, the owner has two choices: get rid of the dog or train him. It is strongly urged that you choose the latter option.

Occasionally there are no classes available within a reasonable distance from the owner's home. Sometimes there are classes available but the tuition is too costly.

Golden Retriever puppies possess great willingness to please the humans who surround them. It is easier to train a puppy that has been loved and socialised.

hesitant, even anxious, about the approach of a stranger, he will respond accordingly.

Once the puppy begins to produce hormones, his natural curiosity emerges and he begins to investigate the world around him. It is at this time when you may notice that the

TRAINING TIP

Stand up straight and authoritatively when giving your dog commands. Do not issue commands when lying on the floor or lying on your back on the sofa. If you are on your hands and knees when you give a command, your dog will think you are positioning yourself to play.

Bonding with a puppy has many benefits. Goldens would rather play with a human (you!) than with other dogs. Take full advantage of this trait.

Whatever the circumstances, the solution to the problem of lack of lesson availability lies within the pages of this book.

This chapter is devoted to helping you train your Golden Retriever at home. If the recommended procedures are followed faithfully, you may expect positive results that will prove rewarding to both you and your dog.

Whether your new charge is a puppy or a mature adult, the methods of teaching and the

TRAINING TIP
If you want to be successful in training your dog, you have four rules to obey yourself:
1. Develop an understanding of how a dog thinks.
2. Do not blame the dog for lack of communication.
3. Define your dog's personality and act accordingly.
4. Have patience and be consistent.

TRAINING TIP
Do not carry your dog to his toilet area. Lead him there on a leash or, better yet, encourage him to follow

you to the spot. If you start carrying him to his spot, you might end up doing this routine forever and your dog will have the satisfaction of having trained YOU.

techniques we use in training basic behaviours are the same. After all, no dog, whether puppy or adult, likes harsh or inhumane methods. All creatures, however, respond favourably to gentle motivational methods and sincere praise and encouragement. Now let us get started.

HOUSEBREAKING
You can train a puppy to relieve itself wherever you choose. For example, city dwellers often train their puppies to relieve themselves in the gutter because large plots of grass are not readily available. Suburbanites, on the other hand, usually have gardens to accommodate their dogs' needs.

Outdoor training includes such surfaces as grass, dirt and cement. Indoor training usually means training your dog to newspaper.

When deciding on the surface and location that you will want your Golden Retriever to use, be sure it is going to be permanent. Training your dog to grass and then changing your mind two months later is extremely difficult for both dog and owner.

Next, choose the command you will use each and every time you want your puppy to void. 'Go hurry up' and 'Go make' are examples of commands commonly used by dog owners.

Get in the habit of asking the puppy, 'Do you want to go hurry up?' (or whatever your chosen relief command is) before you take him out. That way, when he becomes an adult, you will be able to determine if he wants to go out when you ask him. A confirmation will be signs of interest, wagging his tail,

Housebreaking can begin at the breeder's home. A Golden puppy quickly learns the texture of his relief area and will continue to search for it when the time comes. Your breeder can advise you on how to complete the process.

watching you intently, going to the door, etc.

PUPPY'S NEEDS

Puppy needs to relieve himself after play periods, after each meal, after he has been sleeping and any time he indicates that he is looking for a place to urinate or defecate.

The urinary and intestinal tract muscles of very young puppies are not fully developed. Therefore, like human babies, puppies need

DID YOU KNOW?

Dogs will do anything for your attention. If you reward the dog when he is calm and resting, you will develop a well-mannered dog. If, on the other hand, you greet your dog excitedly and encourage him to wrestle and roughhouse with you, the dog will greet you the same way and you will have a hyper dog on your hands.

to relieve themselves frequently.

Take your puppy out often—every hour for an eight-week-old, for example. The older the puppy, the less often he will need to relieve himself. Finally, as a mature healthy adult, he will require only three to five relief trips per day.

HOUSING

Since the types of housing and control you provide for your puppy has a direct relationship on the success of housetraining, we consider the various aspects of both before we begin training.

Bringing a new puppy home and turning him loose in your house can be compared to turning a child loose in a sports arena and telling the child that the place is all his! The sheer enormity of the place would be too much for him to handle.

It's advisable to walk the puppy to his designated area on a lead. A puppy will do his best to tell you when it's time to go out. It's up to you to recognise his body language.

TRAINING TIP
Play fetch games with your dog in an enclosed area where he can retrieve his toy and bring it back to you. Always use

a toy or object designated just for this purpose. Never use a shoe, sock or other item he may later confuse with those in your closet or underneath your chair.

Instead, offer the puppy clearly defined areas where he can play, sleep, eat and live. A room of the house where the family gathers is the most obvious choice. Puppies are social animals and need to feel a part of the pack right from the start. Hearing your voice, watching you whilst you are doing things and smelling you nearby are all positive reinforcers that he is now a member of your pack. Usually a family room, the kitchen or a nearby adjoining breakfast nook is ideal for providing safety and security for both puppy and owner.

Within that room there should be a smaller area

which the puppy can call his own. A cubbyhole, a wire or fibreglass dog crate or a fenced (not boarded!) corner from which he can view the activities of his new family will be fine. The size of the area or crate is the key factor here. The area must be large enough for the puppy to lay down and stretch out as well as stand up without rubbing his head on the top, yet small enough so that he cannot relieve himself at one end and sleep at the other without coming into contact with his droppings.

Dogs are, by nature, clean animals and will not remain close to their relief areas unless

DID YOU KNOW?
By providing sleeping and resting quarters that fit the dog, and offering frequent opportunities to relieve himself outside his quarters, the puppy quickly learns that the outdoors (or the newspaper if you are training him to paper) is the place to go when he needs to urinate or defecate. It also reinforces his innate desire to keep his sleeping quarters clean. This, in turn, helps develop the muscle control that will eventually produce a dog with clean living habits.

forced to do so. In those cases, they then become dirty dogs and usually remain that way for life.

The crate or cubby should be lined with a clean towel and offer one toy, no more. Do not put food or water in the crate, as eating and drinking will activate his digestive processes and ultimately defeat your purpose as well as make the puppy very uncomfortable as he attempts to 'hold it.'

TRAINING TIP
The puppy should also have regular play and exercise sessions when he is with you or a family member. Exercise for a very young puppy can consist of a

short walk around the house or garden. Playing can include fetching games with a large ball or a special raggy. (All puppies teethe and need soft things upon which to chew.) Remember to restrict play periods to indoors within his living area (the family room for example) until he is completely housetrained.

DID YOU KNOW?
If you have other pets in the home and/or interact often with the pets of friends and other family members, your pup will respond to those pets in much the same manner as you do. It is only when you show fear or resentment toward another animal that he will act fearful or unfriendly.

CONTROL
By control, we mean helping the puppy to create a lifestyle pattern that will be compatible to that of his human pack (YOU!). Just as we guide little children to learn our way of life, we must show the puppy when it is time to play, eat, sleep, exercise and even entertain himself.

Your puppy should always sleep in his crate. He should also learn that, during times of household confusion and excessive human activity such as at breakfast when family members are preparing for the day, he can play by himself in relative safety and comfort in his crate. Each time you leave the puppy alone, he should be crated. Puppies are chewers. They cannot tell the difference between lamp cords, television wires, shoes, table legs, etc. Chewing into a television

Canine Development Schedule

It is important to understand how and at what age a puppy develops into adulthood. If you are a puppy owner, consult the following Canine Development Schedule to determine the stage of development your Golden Retriever puppy is currently experiencing. This knowledge will help you as you work with the puppy in the weeks and months ahead.

Period	Age	Characteristics
FIRST TO THIRD	BIRTH TO SEVEN WEEKS	Puppy needs food, sleep and warmth, and responds to simple and gentle touching. Needs mother for security and disciplining. Needs litter mates for learning and interacting with other dogs. Pup learns to function within a pack and learns pack order of dominance. Begin socialising with adults and children for short periods. Begins to become aware of its environment.
FOURTH	EIGHT TO TWELVE WEEKS	Brain is fully developed. Needs socialising with outside world. Remove from mother and littermates. Needs to change from canine pack to human pack. Human dominance necessary. Fear period occurs between 8 and 16 weeks. Avoid fright and pain.
FIFTH	THIRTEEN TO SIXTEEN WEEKS	Training and formal obedience should begin. Less association with other dogs, more with people, places, situations. Period will pass easily if you remember this is pup's change-to-adolescence time. Be firm and fair. Flight instinct prominent. Permissiveness and over-disciplining can do permanent damage. Praise for good behaviour.
JUVENILE	FOUR TO EIGHT MONTHS	Another fear period about 7 to 8 months of age. It passes quickly, but be cautious of fright and pain. Sexual maturity reached. Dominant traits established. Dog should understand sit, down, come and stay by now.

NOTE: THESE ARE APPROXIMATE TIME FRAMES. ALLOW FOR INDIVIDUAL DIFFERENCES IN PUPPIES.

wire, for example, can be fatal to the puppy whilst a shorted wire can start a fire in the house.

If the puppy chews on the arm of the chair when he is alone, you will probably discipline him angrily when you get home. Thus, he makes the association that your coming home means he is going to be hit or punished. (He will not remember chewing up the chair and is incapable of making the association of the discipline with his naughty deed.)

DID YOU KNOW?

Never line your pup's sleeping area with newspaper. Puppy litters are usually raised on newspaper and, once in your home, the puppy will immediately associate newspaper with voiding.

Never put newspaper on any floor while housetraining, as this will only confuse the puppy. If you are paper-training him, use paper in his designated relief area ONLY. Finally, restrict water intake after evening meals. Offer a few licks at a time—never let a young puppy gulp water after meals.

Other times of excitement, such as family parties, etc., can be fun for the puppy providing he can view the activities from the security of his crate. He is not underfoot and he is not being fed all sorts of titbits that will probably cause him stomach distress, yet he still feels a part of the fun.

SCHEDULE

A puppy should be taken to his relief area each time he is released from his crate, after meals, after a play session, when he first awakens in the morning (at age eight weeks, this can mean 5 a.m.!). The puppy will indicate that he's ready 'to go' by circling or sniffing busily—do not misinterpret these signs. For a puppy less than ten weeks of age, a routine of taking him out every hour is necessary. As the puppy grows, he will be able to wait for longer periods of time.

Keep trips to his relief area short. Stay no more than five or six minutes and then return to the house. If he goes during that time, praise him lavishly and take him indoors immediately. If he does not, but he has an accident when you go back indoors, pick him up immediately, say 'No! No!' and return to his relief area. Wait a few minutes, then return to the house again. never hit a puppy or rub his face in urine or excrement when he has an accident!

Once indoors, put the puppy in his crate until you have had time to clean up his accident. Then release him to the family area and watch him more closely than before. Chances are, his accident was a result of your not picking up his signal or waiting too long before offering him the opportunity to relieve himself. Never hold a grudge against the puppy for accidents.

Let the puppy learn that going outdoors means it is time to relieve himself, not play. Once trained, he will be able to play indoors and out and still differentiate between the times for play versus the times for relief.

Help him develop regular hours for naps, being alone, playing by himself and just resting, all in his crate. Encourage him to entertain himself whilst you are busy with your activities. Let him learn that having you near is

HOW MANY TIMES A DAY?	
AGE	RELIEF TRIPS
To 14 weeks	10
14–22 weeks	8
22–32 weeks	6
Adulthood (dog stops growing)	4

These are estimates, of course, but they are a guide to the MINIMUM opportunities a dog should have each day to relieve itself.

comforting, but it is not your main purpose in life to provide him with undivided attention.

Each time you put a puppy in his crate tell him, 'Crate time!' (or whatever command you choose). Soon, he will run to his crate when he hears you say those words.

In the beginning of his training, do not leave him in his crate for prolonged periods of time except during the night

DID YOU KNOW?

Mealtime should be a peaceful time for your puppy. Do not put his food and water bowls in a high-traffic area in the house. For example, give him his own little corner of the kitchen where he can eat undisturbed and where he will not be under foot. Do not allow small children or other family members to disrupt the pup when he is eating.

Ideally your Golden puppy will find and mark a place that he will always use to relieve himself. If there is an area of your garden that you do not want him to use, it's best to deny him access.

when everyone is sleeping. Make his experience with his crate a pleasant one and, as an adult, he will love his crate and willingly stay in it for several hours. There are millions of people who go to work every day and leave their adult dogs crated whilst they are away. The dogs accept this as their lifestyle and look forward to 'crate time.'

Crate training provides safety for you, the puppy and the home. It also provides the puppy with a feeling of security, and that helps the puppy achieve self-confidence and clean habits.

Remember that one of the primary ingredients in housetraining your puppy is control. Regardless of your lifestyle, there will always be occasions when you will need to have a place where your dog can stay and be happy and safe. Crate training is the answer for now and in the future.

In conclusion, a few key elements are really all you need for a successful house and crate training method—consistency, frequency,

DID YOU KNOW?
Do not use a choke collar on a dog under four months of age. Choke collars are for training only and should be removed after the lessons or exercises.

praise, control and supervision. By following these procedures with a normal, healthy puppy, you and the puppy will soon be past the stage of 'accidents' and ready to move on to a full and rewarding life together.

ROLES OF DISCIPLINE, REWARD AND PUNISHMENT

Discipline, training one to act in accordance with rules, brings order to life. It is as simple as that. Without discipline, particularly in a group society, chaos reigns supreme and the group will eventually perish. Humans and canines are social animals and need some form of discipline in order to function effectively. They must procure food, protect their home base and their young and reproduce to keep the species going.

If there were no discipline in the lives of social animals, they would eventually die from starvation and/or predation by other stronger animals.

THE SUCCESS METHOD
6 Steps to Successful Crate Training

1 Tell the puppy 'Crate time!' and place him in the crate with a small treat (a piece of cheese or half of a biscuit). Let him stay in the crate for five minutes while you are in the same room. Then release him and praise lavishly. Never release him when he is fussing. Wait until he is quiet before you let him out.

2 Repeat Step 1 several times a day.

3 The next day, place the puppy in the crate as before. Let him stay there for ten minutes. Do this several times.

4 Continue building time in five-minute increments until the puppy stays in his crate for 30 minutes with you in the room. Always take him to his relief area after prolonged periods in his crate.

5 Now go back to Step 1 and let the puppy stay in his crate for five minutes, this time while you are out of the room.

6 Once again, build crate time in five-minute increments with you out of the room. When the puppy will stay willingly in his crate (he may even fall asleep!) for 30 minutes with you out of the room, he will be ready to stay in it for several hours at a time.

In the case of domestic canines, dogs need discipline in their lives in order to understand how their pack (you and other family members) functions and how they must act in order to survive.

A large humane society in a highly populated area recently surveyed dog owners regarding their satisfaction with their relationships with their dogs. People who had trained their dogs were 75% more satisfied with their pets than those who had never trained their dogs.

Dr. Edward Thorndike, a psychologist, established *Thorndike's Theory of Learning*, which states that a

DID YOU KNOW?
Golden Retrievers are known to be 'soft' dogs who learn best with gentle teaching. A Golden thrives on praise and knowing he has pleased his person.

Never physically abuse your dog or hit him with your hand, foot, newspaper or other object. That will only teach the dog to be afraid of you.

TRAINING TIP
Practice Makes Perfect!
• Have training lessons with your dog every day in several short segments—three to five times a day for a few minutes at a time is ideal.
  • Do not have long practice sessions. The dog will become easily bored.
  • Never practice when you are tired, ill, worried or in an otherwise negative mood. This will transmit to the dog and may have an adverse effect on its performance.
  Think fun, short and above all POSITIVE! End each session on a high note, rather than a failed exercise, and make sure to give a lot of praise. Enjoy the training and help your dog enjoy it, too.

behaviour that results in a pleasant event tends to be repeated. A behaviour that results in an unpleasant event tends not to be repeated. It is this theory on which training methods are based today. For example, if you manipulate a dog to perform a specific behaviour and reward him for doing it, he is likely to do it

Dogs need discipline as well as love and companionship.

TRAINING EQUIPMENT
COLLAR

A simple buckle collar is fine for most dogs. One who pulls mightily on the leash may require a chain choker collar. Only in the most severe cases of a dog being totally out of control is the use of a prong or

Pleasant events tend to be repeated.

pinch collar recommended. These collars should only be used by owners with experience in the proper use of such equipment. In some areas, such as the United Kingdom, these types of collars are not allowed.

again because he enjoyed the end result.

Occasionally, punishment, a penalty inflicted for an offence, is necessary. The best type of punishment often comes from an outside source. For example, a child is told not to touch the stove because he may get burned. He disobeys and touches the stove. In doing so, he receives a burn. From that time on, he respects the heat of the stove and avoids contact with it. Therefore, a behaviour that results in an unpleasant event tends not to be repeated.

A good example of a dog learning the hard way is the dog who chases the house cat. He is told many times to leave the cat alone, yet he persists in teasing the cat. Then, one day he begins chasing the cat but the cat turns and swipes a claw across the dog's face, leaving him with a painful gash on his nose. The final result is that the dog stops chasing the cat.

DID YOU KNOW?

Dogs do not understand our language. They can be trained to react to a certain sound, at a certain volume. If you say 'No, Oliver' in a very soft pleasant voice it will not have the same meaning as 'No, Oliver!!' when you shout it as loud as you can. You should never use the dog's name during a reprimand, just the command NO!! Since dogs don't understand words, comics use dogs trained with opposite meanings. Thus, when the comic commands his dog to SIT the dog will stand up; and vice versa.

CHOOSE AN APPROPRIATE COLLAR

The **BUCKLE COLLAR** is the standard collar used for everyday purposes. Be sure that you adjust the buckle on growing puppies. Check it every day. It can become too tight overnight! These collars can be made of leather or nylon. Attach your dog's identification tags to this collar.

The **CHOKE COLLAR** is constructed of highly polished steel so that it slides easily through the stainless steel loop. The idea is that the dog controls the pressure around his neck and he will stop pulling if the collar becomes uncomfortable. It is used *only* for training and should *never* be left on a dog.

The **HALTER** is for a trained dog that has to be restrained to prevent running away, chasing a cat and the like. Considered the most humane of all collars, it is frequently used on smaller dogs on which collars are not comfortable.

LEAD

A 1- to 2-metre lead is recommended, preferably made of leather, nylon or heavy cloth. A chain lead is not recommended, as many dog owners find that the chain cuts into their hands and that frequently switching the lead back and forth between their hands is painful.

TREATS

Have a bag of treats on hand. Something nutritious and easy to swallow works best. Use a soft treat, a chunk of cheese or a piece of cooked chicken rather than a dry biscuit. By the time the dog gets done chewing a dry treat, he will forget why he is being rewarded in the first place! Using food rewards will not teach a dog to beg at the table—the only way to teach a dog to beg at the table is to give him food from the table. In training, rewarding the dog with a food treat will help him associate praise and the treats with learning new behaviours that obviously please his owner.

TRAINING BEGINS: ASK THE DOG A QUESTION

In order to teach your dog anything, you must first get his attention. After all, he cannot learn anything if he is looking away from you with his mind on something else.

To get his attention, ask him, 'School?' and immediately walk over to him and give him a treat as you tell him 'Good dog.' Wait a minute or two and repeat the routine, this time with a treat in your hand as you approach within a foot of the dog. Do not go directly to him, but stop about a foot

Your local pet shop usually has a wide variety of leads from which you can make your own choice.

short of him and hold out the treat as you ask, 'School?' He will see you approaching with a treat in your hand and most likely begin walking toward you. As you meet, give him the treat and praise again.

95

If your Golden Retriever has received training throughout its life by various members of the family, it will respond positively to both children and adults.

The third time, ask the question, have a treat in your hand and walk only a short distance toward the dog so that he must walk almost all the way to you. As he reaches you, give him the treat and praise again.

By this time, the dog will probably be getting the idea that if he pays attention to you, especially when you ask that question, it will pay off in treats and fun activities for him. In

Once your Golden is sufficiently trained, you can practise your commands and incorporate a favourite game into the sessions.

other words, he learns that 'school' means doing fun things with you that result in treats and positive attention for him.

Remember that the dog does not understand your verbal language, he only recognises sounds. Your question translates to a series of sounds for him, and those sounds become the signal to go to you and pay attention; if he does, he will get to interact with you plus receive treats and praise.

THE BASIC COMMANDS
TEACHING SIT

Now that you have the dog's attention, attach his lead and hold it in your left hand and a food treat in your right. Place your food hand at the dog's nose and let him lick the treat but not take it from you. Say 'Sit' and slowly raise your food hand from in front of the dog's nose up over his head so that he is looking at the ceiling. As he bends his head upward, he will have to bend his knees to maintain his balance. As he bends his knees, he will assume a sit position. At that point, release the food treat and praise

TEACHING DOWN

Teaching the down exercise is easy when you understand how the dog perceives the down position, and it is very difficult when you do not. Dogs perceive the down position as a submissive one, therefore teaching the down exercise using a forceful method can sometimes make the dog develop such a fear of the down that he either runs away when you say 'Down' or he attempts to bite the person who tries to force him down.

Have the dog sit close alongside your left leg, facing in the same direction as you are. Hold the lead in your left hand and a food treat in your right. Now place your left hand lightly on the top of the dog's shoulders where they meet above the spinal cord.

Since most Goldens love to eat, using food rewards is an absolutely fool-proof way to train this breed.

lavishly with comments such as 'Good dog! Good sit!', etc. Remember to always praise enthusiastically, because dogs relish verbal praise from their owners and feel so proud of themselves whenever they accomplish a behaviour.

You will not use food forever in getting the dog to obey your commands. Food is only used to teach new behaviours, and once the dog knows what you want when you give a specific command, you will wean him off of the food treats but still maintain the verbal praise. After all, you will always have your voice with you, and there will be many times when you have no food rewards but expect the dog to obey.

DID YOU KNOW?

Success that comes by luck is usually short lived. Success that comes by well-thought-out proven methods is often more easily achieved and permanent. This is the Success Method. It is designed to give you, the puppy owner, a simple yet proven way to help your puppy develop clean living habits and a feeling of security in his new environment.

Shaking hands is amongst the most common tricks to teach your dog. Goldens are naturally very friendly and happy to lend a paw.

Do not push down on the dog's shoulders; simply rest your left hand there so you can guide the dog to lie down close to your left leg rather than to swing away from your side when he drops.

Now place the food hand at the dog's nose, say 'Down' very softly (almost a whisper), and slowly lower the food hand to the dog's front feet. When the food hand reaches the floor, begin moving it forward along the floor in front of the dog. Keep talking softly to the dog,

You can train your Golden Retriever to retrieve almost anything! It's better to use a retrieving dummy or a toy than a natural tree branch, which might have been treated with a toxic insecticide.

saying things like, 'Do you want this treat? You can do this, good dog.' Your reassuring tone of voice will help calm the dog as he tries to follow the food hand in order to get the treat.

When the dog's elbows touch the floor, release the food and praise softly. Try to get the dog to maintain that down position for several seconds before you let him sit up again. The goal here is to get the dog to settle down and not feel threatened in the down position.

TEACHING STAY

It is easy to teach the dog to stay in either a sit or a down position. Again, we use food and praise during the teaching process as we help the dog to understand exactly what it is that we are expecting him to do.

To teach the sit/stay, start with the dog sitting on your left side as before and hold the lead in your left hand. Have a food treat in your right hand and place your food hand at the dog's nose. Say 'Stay' and step out on your right foot to stand directly in front of the

TRAINING TIP

A dog in jeopardy never lies down. He stays alert on his feet because instinct tells him that he may have to run away or fight for his survival. Therefore, if a dog feels threatened or anxious, he will not lie down. Consequently, it is important to have the dog calm and relaxed as he learns the down exercise.

dog, toe to toe, as he licks and nibbles the treat. Be sure to keep his head facing upward to maintain the sit position. Count to five and then swing around to stand next to the dog again with him on your left. As soon as you get back to the original position, release the food and praise lavishly.

To teach the down/stay, do the down as previously described. As soon as the dog lies down, say 'Stay' and step out on your right foot just as you did in the sit/stay. Count to five and then return to stand beside the dog with him on your left side. Release the treat and praise as always.

Within a week or ten days, you can begin to add a bit of distance between you and your dog when you leave him. When you do, use your left hand open with the palm facing the dog as a stay signal, much the same as the hand signal a police officer uses to stop traffic at an intersection. Hold the food treat in your right hand as before, but this time the food is not touching the dog's nose. He will watch the food hand and quickly learn that he is going to get that treat as soon as you return to his side.

When you can stand 1 metre away from your dog for 30 seconds, you can then begin

Teaching a dog to sit/stay is easy when you use food and praise in the teaching process.

building time and distance in both stays. Eventually, the dog can be expected to remain in the stay position for prolonged periods of time until you return to him or call him to you. Always praise lavishly when he stays.

TEACHING COME
If you make teaching 'come' a fun experience, you should never have a 'student' that does not love the game or that fails to come when called. The secret, it seems, is never to teach the word 'come.'

TRAINING TIP

When calling the dog, do not say 'Come.' Say things like, 'Rover, where are you? See if you can find me! I have a cookie for you!' Keep up a constant line of chatter with coaxing sounds and frequent questions such as, 'Where are you?' The dog will learn to follow the sound of your voice to locate you and receive his reward.

At times when an owner most wants his dog to come when called, the owner is likely upset or anxious and he allows these feelings to come through in the tone of his voice when he calls his dog. Hearing that desperation in his owner's voice, the dog fears the results of going to him and therefore either disobeys outright or runs in the opposite direction. The secret, therefore, is to teach the dog a game and, when you want him to come to you, simply play the game. It is practically a no-fail solution!

To begin, have several members of your family take a few food treats and each go into a different room in the house. Take turns calling the dog, and each person should celebrate the dog's finding him with a treat and lots of happy praise. When a person calls the dog, he is actually inviting the dog to find him and get a treat as a reward for 'winning.'

A few turns of the 'Where are you?' game and the dog will figure out that everyone is playing the game and that each person has a big celebration awaiting his success at locating them. Once he learns to love the game, simply calling out 'Where are you?' will bring

When teaching your Golden to *Come*, never use the word 'come'.

DID YOU KNOW?

Never call your dog to come to you for a correction or scold him when he reaches you. That is the quickest way to turn a 'Come' command into 'Go away fast!' Dogs think only in the present tense and he will connect the scolding with coming to his master, not with the misbehaviour of a few moments earlier.

him running from wherever he is when he hears that all-important question.

The come command is recognised as one of the most important things to teach a dog, but there are trainers who work with thousands of dogs and never teach the actual word 'Come.' Yet these dogs will race to respond to a person who uses the dog's name followed by 'Where are you?' For example, a woman has a 12-year-old companion dog who went blind, but who never fails to locate her owner when asked, 'Where are you?'

Children particularly love to play this game with their dogs. Children can hide in smaller places like a shower or bathtub, behind a bed or under a table. The dog needs to work a little bit harder to find these hiding places, but when he does he loves to celebrate with a treat and a tussle with a favourite youngster.

TEACHING HEEL

Heeling means that the dog walks beside the owner without pulling. It takes time and patience on the owner's part to succeed at teaching the dog that he (the owner) will not proceed unless the dog is walking calmly beside him. Pulling out ahead on the lead is definitely not acceptable.

Begin with holding the lead in your left hand as the dog sits beside your left leg. Move the loop end of the lead to your right hand but keep

Your Golden is what you make him. He can be a trained pet or an ill-behaved nuisance.

your left hand short on the lead so it keeps the dog in close next to you.

Say 'Heel' and step forward on your left foot. Keep the dog close to you and take three steps. Stop and have the dog sit next to you in what we now call the 'heel position.' Praise verbally, but do not touch the

TRAINING TIP

If you are walking your dog and he suddenly stops and looks straight into your eyes, ignore him. Pull the leash and lead him into the direction you want to walk.

Your Golden must be trained to *Heel*. He should remain close to your side and anticipate your next command.

dog.' The 'OK' is used as a release word meaning that the exercise is finished and the dog is free to relax.

If you are dealing with a dog who insists on pulling you around, simply 'put on your brakes' and stand your ground until the dog realises that the two of you are not going anywhere until he is beside you and moving at your pace, not his. It may take some time just standing there to convince the dog that you are the leader and you will be the one to decide on the direction and speed of your travel.

Each time the dog looks up at you or slows down to give a slack lead between the two of you, quietly praise him and say, 'Good heel. Good dog.' Eventually, the dog will begin to respond and within a few days he will be walking politely beside you without pulling on the lead. At first, the training sessions should be kept short and very positive; soon the dog will be able to walk nicely with you for

dog. Hesitate a moment and begin again with 'Heel,' taking three steps and stopping, at which point the dog is told to sit again.

Your goal here is to have the dog walk those three steps without pulling on the lead. When he will walk calmly beside you for three steps without pulling, increase the number of steps you take to five. When he will walk politely beside you whilst you take five steps, you can increase the length of your walk to ten steps. Keep increasing the length of your stroll until the dog will walk quietly beside you without pulling as long as you want him to heel. When you stop heeling, indicate to the dog that the exercise is over by verbally praising as you pet him and say 'OK, good

TRAINING TIP
Teach your dog to HEEL in an enclosed area. Once you think the dog will obey reliably and you want to attempt advanced obedience exercises such as off-lead heeling, test him in a fenced in area so he cannot run away.

TRAINING TIP

Dogs are sensitive to their master's moods and emotions. Use your voice wisely when communicating with your dog. Never raise your voice at your dog unless you are angry and trying to correct him. 'Barking' at your dog can become as meaningless as 'dogspeak' is to you. Think before you bark!

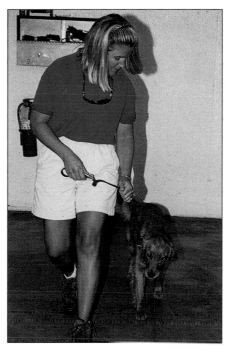

Heel training requires constant repetition and experience. Start the training indoors, if possible, where there are few distractions like other people or vehicles. Goldens make excellent guides for the vision-impaired. This Golden is being trained at The Seeing Eye®, Morristown, NJ, USA.

increasingly longer distances. Remember also to give the dog free time and the opportunity to run and play when you are done with heel practice.

WEANING OFF FOOD IN TRAINING

Food is used in training new behaviours. Once the dog understands what behaviour goes with a specific command, it is time to start weaning him off the food treats. At first, give a treat after each exercise. Then, start to give a treat only after every other exercise. Mix up the times when you offer a food reward and the times when you only offer praise so that the dog will never know when he is going to receive both food and praise and when he is going to receive only praise. This is called a variable ratio reward system and it proves successful because there is always the chance that the owner will produce a treat, so the dog never stops trying

for that reward. No matter what, ALWAYS give verbal praise.

OBEDIENCE CLASSES

As previously discussed, it is a good idea to enrol in an obedience class if one is available in your area. Many

TRAINING TIP

If you begin teaching the heel by taking long walks and letting the dog pull you along, he misinterprets this action as an acceptable form of taking a walk. When you pull back on the lead to counteract his pulling, he reads that tug as a signal to pull even harder!

areas have dog clubs that offer basic obedience training as well as preparatory classes for obedience competition. There are also local dog trainers who offer similar classes.

At obedience trials, dogs can earn titles at various levels of competition. The beginning levels of competition include basic behaviours such as sit, down, heel, etc. The more advanced levels of competition include jumping, retrieving, scent discrimination and signal work. The advanced levels require a dog and owner to put a lot of time and effort into their training and the titles that can be earned at these levels of competition are very prestigious.

OTHER ACTIVITIES FOR LIFE

Whether a dog is trained in the structured environment of a

> **DID YOU KNOW?**
> To a dog's way of thinking, your hands are like his mouth in terms of a defence mechanism. If you squeeze him too tightly, he might just bite you because that would be his normal response. This is not aggressive biting and, although all biting should be discouraged, you need the discipline in learning how to handle your dog.

class or alone with his owner at home, there are many activities that can bring fun and rewards to both owner and dog once they have mastered basic control.

Teaching the dog to help out around the home, in the garden or on the farm provides great satisfaction to both dog and owner. In addition, the dog's help makes life a little easier for his owner and raises his stature as a valued companion to his family. It helps give the dog a purpose by occupying his mind and

> **DID YOU KNOW?**
> A basic obedience beginner's class usually lasts for six to eight weeks. Dog and owner attend an hour-long lesson once a week and practice for a few minutes, several times a day, each day at home. If done properly, the whole procedure will result in a well-mannered dog and an owner who delights in living with a pet that is eager to please and enjoys doing things with his owner.

> **DID YOU KNOW?**
> Training a dog is a life experience. Many parents admit that much of what they know about raising children they learned from caring for their dogs. Dogs respond to love, fairness and guidance, just as children do. Become a good dog owner and you may become an even better parent.

providing an outlet for his energy.

Backpacking is an exciting and healthful activity that the dog can be taught without assistance from more than his owner. The exercise of walking and climbing is good for man and dog alike, and the bond that they develop together is priceless.

If you are interested in participating in organised competition with your Golden Retriever, there are activities other than obedience in which you and your dog can become involved. Agility is a popular and fun sport where dogs run through an obstacle course that includes various jumps, tunnels and other exercises to test the dog's speed and coordination. The owners often run through the course beside their dogs to give commands and to guide them through the course. Although competitive, the focus is on fun—it's fun to do, fun to watch, and great exercise.

Golden Retrievers can accomplish anything they are trained to do. Few breeds have the trainability and adaptability of the Golden. Here's a Golden backpacking on holiday.

DID YOU KNOW?
Occasionally, a dog and owner who have not attended formal classes have been able to earn entry-level titles by obtaining competition rules and regulations from a local kennel club and practising on their own to a degree of perfection. Obtaining the higher level titles, however, almost always requires extensive training under the tutelage of experienced instructors. In addition, the more difficult levels require more specialised equipment whereas the lower levels do not.

First Aid
at a Glance

Burns

Place the affected area under cool water; use ice if only a small area is burnt.

Car accident

Move dog from roadway with blanket; seek veterinary aid.

Bee/Insect bites

Apply ice to relieve swelling; antihistamine dosed properly.

Shock

Calm the dog, keep him warm; seek immediate veterinary help.

Animal bites

Clean any bleeding area; apply pressure until bleeding subsides; go to the vet.

Nosebleed

Apply cold compress to the nose; apply pressure to any visible abrasion.

Spider bites

Use cold compress and a pressurised pack to inhibit venom's spreading.

Bleeding

Apply pressure above the area; treat wound by applying a cotton pack.

Antifreeze poisoning

Immediately induce vomiting by using hydrogen peroxide.

Heat stroke

Submerge dog in cold bath; cool down with fresh air and water; go to the vet.

Fish hooks

Removal best handled by vet; hook must be cut in order to remove.

Frostbite/Hypothermia

Warm the dog with a warm bath, electric blankets or hot water bottles.

Snake bites

Pack ice around bite; contact vet quickly; identify snake for proper antivenin.

Abrasions

Clean the wound and wash out thoroughly with fresh water; apply antiseptic.

 Remember: an injured dog may attempt to bite a helping hand from fear and confusion. Always muzzle the dog before trying to offer assistance.

Golden Retriever

Dogs suffer many of the same physical illnesses as people. They might even share many of the same psychological problems. Since people usually know more about human diseases than canine maladies, many of the terms used in this chapter will be familiar but not necessarily those used by veterinary surgeons. We will use the term x-ray, instead of the more acceptable term radiograph. We will also use the familiar term symptoms even though dogs don't have symptoms, which are verbal descriptions of the patient's feelings: dogs have clinical signs. Since dogs can't speak, we have to look for clinical signs...but we still use the term symptoms in this book.

As a general rule, medicine is practised. That term is not arbitrary. Medicine is a constantly changing art as we learn more and more about genetics, electronic aids (like CAT scans) and daily laboratory advances. There are many dog maladies, like canine hip dysplasia, which are not universally treated in the same manner. Some veterinary surgeons opt for surgery more often than others do.

SELECTING A VETERINARY SURGEON

Your selection of a veterinary surgeon should not be based upon personality (as most are) but upon their convenience to your home. You want a doctor who is close because you might have emergencies or need to make multiple visits for treatments. You want a doctor who has services that you might require such as a boarding kennel and grooming facilities, as well as sophisticated pet

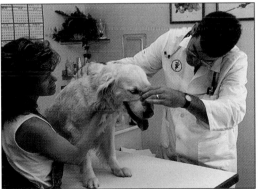

Never compromise in your selection of a veterinary surgeon. Find a vet who offers the services you need and with whom you feel comfortable.

supplies and a good reputation for ability and responsiveness. There is nothing more frustrating than having to wait a day or more to get a response from your veterinary surgeon.

107

All veterinary surgeons are licensed and their diplomas and/or certificates should be displayed in their waiting rooms. There are, however, many veterinary specialties that usually require further studies and internships. There are specialists in heart problems (veterinary cardiologists), skin problems (veterinary dermatolo-

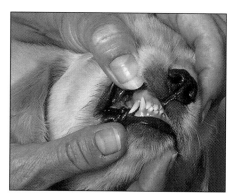

Your Golden Retriever's teeth should be checked regularly by your veterinary surgeon.

gists), teeth and gum problems (veterinary dentists), eye problems (veterinary ophthalmologists), x-rays (veterinary radiologists), and surgeons who have specialties in bones, muscles or other organs. Most veterinary surgeons do routine surgery such as neutering, stitching up wounds and docking tails for those breeds in which such is required for show purposes. When the problem affecting your dog is serious, it is not unusual or impudent to get another medical opinion. You might also want to compare

costs amongst several veterinary surgeons. Sophisticated health care and veterinary services can be very costly. Don't be bashful about discussing these costs with your veterinary surgeon or his (her) staff. It is not infrequent that important decisions are based upon financial considerations.

PREVENTATIVE MEDICINE

It is much easier, less costly and more effective to practise preventative medicine than to fight bouts of illness and disease. Properly bred puppies come from parents that were selected based upon their genetic disease profile. Their mothers should have been vaccinated, free of all internal and external parasites, and properly nourished. For these reasons, a visit to the veterinary surgeon who cared for the dam (mother) is recommended. The dam can pass on disease resistance to her puppies, which can last for eight to ten weeks. She can also pass on parasites and many infections. That's why you should visit the veterinary surgeon who cared for the dam.

WEANING TO FIVE MONTHS OLD

Puppies should be weaned by the time they are about two months old. A puppy that remains for at least eight weeks with its mother and litter mates

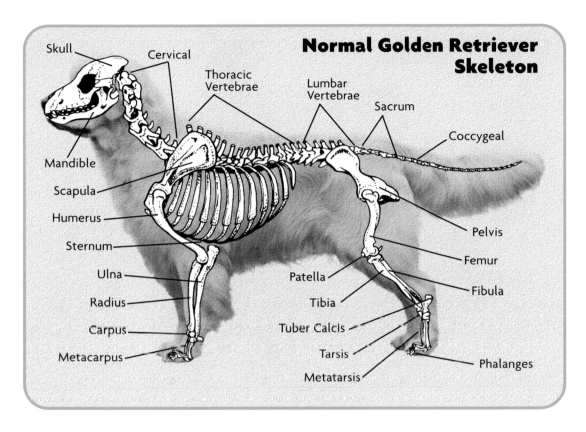

Normal Golden Retriever Skeleton

Skull
Cervical
Thoracic Vertebrae
Lumbar Vertebrae
Sacrum
Coccygeal
Mandible
Scapula
Humerus
Sternum
Ulna
Radius
Carpus
Metacarpus
Patella
Tibia
Tuber Calcis
Tarsis
Metatarsis
Pelvis
Femur
Fibula
Phalanges

usually adapts better to other dogs and people later in its life.

In every case, you should have your newly acquired puppy examined by a veterinary surgeon immediately. Vaccination programmes usually begin when the puppy is very young.

The puppy will have its teeth examined and have its skeletal conformation and general health checked prior to certification by the veterinary surgeon. Many puppies have problems with their kneecaps, eye cataracts and other eye problems, heart murmurs and undescended testicles. They may also have personality problems and your veterinary surgeon might have training in temperament evaluation.

VACCINATION SCHEDULING
Most vaccinations are given by injection and should only be done by a veterinary surgeon. Both he and you should keep a record of the date of the

109

HEALTH AND VACCINATION SCHEDULE

Age in Weeks:	3rd	6th	8th	10th	12th	14th	16th	20-24th
Worm Control	✔	✔	✔	✔	✔	✔	✔	✔
Neutering								✔
Heartworm*		✔						✔
Parvovirus		✔		✔		✔		✔
Distemper			✔		✔		✔	
Hepatitis			✔		✔		✔	
Leptospirosis		✔		✔		✔		
Parainfluenza		✔		✔		✔		
Dental Examination			✔					✔
Complete Physical			✔					✔
Temperament Testing			✔					
Coronavirus					✔			
Canine Cough		✔						
Hip Dysplasia							✔	
Rabies*								✔

Vaccinations are not instantly effective. It takes about two weeks for the dog's immunisation system to develop antibodies. Most vaccinations require annual booster shots. Your veterinary surgeon should guide you in this regard.
*Not applicable in the United Kingdom

injection, the identification of the vaccine and the amount given. The first vaccinations should start when the puppy is 6–8 weeks old, the second when it is 10–12 weeks of age and the third when it is 14–16 weeks of age. Vaccinations should never be given without a two- to three-week lapse between injections. Most vaccinations immunise your puppy against viruses.

The usual vaccines contain immunising doses of several different viruses such as distemper, parvovirus, parain-fluenza and hepatitis. There are other vaccines available when the puppy is at risk. You should rely upon professional advice. This is especially true for the booster-shot programme. Most vaccination programmes require a booster when the puppy is a year old and once a year thereafter. In some cases, circumstances may require more frequent immunisations. Canine cough, more formally known as tracheobronchitis, is treated with a vaccine that is sprayed into the dog's nostrils.

The effectiveness of a

parvovirus vaccination programme can be tested using the parvovirus antibody titer to be certain that the vaccinations are protective. Your veterinary surgeon will explain and manage all of these details.

FIVE MONTHS TO ONE YEAR OF AGE

By the time your puppy is five months old, he should have completed his vaccination programme. During his physical examination he should be evaluated for the common hip dysplasia and other diseases of the joints. There are tests to assist in the prediction of these problems. Other tests can be run to assess the effectiveness of the vaccination programme.

Unless you intend to breed or show your dog, neutering the puppy at six months of age is recommended. Discuss this with your veterinary surgeon.

By the time your Golden Retriever is seven or eight months of age, he can be seriously evaluated for his conformation to the club standard, thus determining show potential and desirability as a sire or dam. Of course, desirability as a working dog sire or dam has less to do with the breed standard than it does training and performance. If the puppy is not top class and therefore is not a candidate for a serious breeding programme,

most professionals advise neutering the puppy. Neutering has proven to be extremely beneficial to both male and female puppies. Besides eliminating the possibility of pregnancy, it inhibits (but does not prevent) breast cancer in bitches and prostate cancer in male dogs.

DOGS OLDER THAN ONE YEAR

Continue to visit the veterinary surgeon at least once a year. There is no such disease as old age, but the bodily functions of your dog do change with age.

Together with your vet, you can develop a schedule of vaccinations and routine exams to keep your Golden healthy throughout his life.

DID YOU KNOW?

A dental examination is in order when the dog is between six months and one year of age so any permanent teeth that have erupted incorrectly can be corrected. It is important to begin a brushing routine, preferably using a two-sided brushing technique, whereby both sides of the tooth are brushed at the same time. Durable nylon and safe edible chews should be a part of your puppy's arsenal for good health, good teeth and pleasant breath. The vast majority of dogs three to four years old and older has diseases of their gums from lack of dental attention. Using the various types of dental chews can be very effective in controlling dental plaque.

By the time your dog is a year old, you should have become very comfortable with your local veterinary surgeon and have agreed on scheduled visits for booster vaccinations. Blood tests should now be taken regularly, for comparative purposes, for such variables as cholesterol and triglycerides levels, thyroid hormones, liver enzymes, blood cell counts, etc.

The eyes, ears, nose and throat should be examined regularly and an annual cleaning of the teeth is a ritual. For teeth scaling, the dog must be anaesthetised.

The eyes and ears are no longer as efficient. Liver, kidney and intestinal functions often decline. Proper dietary changes, recommended by your veterinary surgeon, can make life more pleasant for the ageing Golden Retriever and you.

SKIN PROBLEMS IN GOLDEN RETRIEVERS

Veterinary surgeons are consulted by dog owners for skin problems more than any other group of diseases or maladies. Dogs' skin is almost as sensitive as human skin and both suffer almost the same ailments. (Though the occurrence of acne in dogs is rare!) For this reason, veterinary dermatology has developed into a specialty practised by many veterinary surgeons.

Since many skin problems have visual symptoms that are almost identical, it requires the skill of an experienced veterinary dermatologist to identify and cure many of the more severe skin disorders. Pet shops sell many treatments for skin problems but most of the treatments are directed at symptoms and not the underlying problem(s). If your dog is suffering from a skin disorder, you should seek professional assistance as quickly as possible. As with all diseases, the earlier a problem is identified and treated, the more successful is the cure.

PARASITE BITES

Many of us are allergic to mosquito bites. The bites itch, erupt and may even become infected. Dogs have the same reaction to fleas, ticks and/or mites. When you feel the prick of the mosquito as it bites you, you have a chance to kill it with your hand. Unfortunately, when our dog is bitten by a flea, tick or mite, it can only scratch it away or bite it. By the time the dog has been bitten, the parasite has done some of its damage. It may also have laid eggs to cause further problems in the near future. The itching from parasite bites is probably due to the saliva injected into the site when the parasite sucks the dog's blood.

AUTO-IMMUNE SKIN CONDITIONS

Auto-immune skin conditions are commonly referred to as being allergic to yourself, whilst allergies are usually inflammatory reactions to an outside stimulus. Auto-immune diseases cause serious damage to the tissues that are involved.

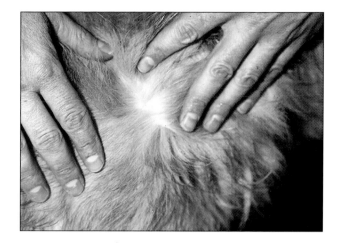

The best known auto-immune disease is lupus, which affects people as well as dogs. The symptoms are variable and may affect the kidneys, bones, blood chemistry and skin. It can be fatal to both dogs and humans, though it is not thought to be transmissible. It is usually successfully treated with cortisone, prednisone or similar corticosteroid, but extensive use of these drugs can have harmful side effects.

You should inspect your Golden's skin regularly looking for rashes and parasites. Hold the hairs apart with your hands and then blow to expose the skin

ACRAL LICK DISEASE

Golden Retrievers and other dogs about the same size (like German Shepherd Dogs), have a very poorly understood syndrome called acral lick. The manifestation of the problem is the dog's tireless attack at a specific area of the body, almost always the legs. They lick so intensively that they remove the hair and skin leaving an ugly, large wound. There is no absolute cure,

As breathtaking as the great outdoors can be, dogs can be affected by parasites, pollen and other problems whilst touring the countryside.

Acral lick
granuloma,
similar to a hot
spot, is of
undefined origin.
The dog
constantly licks
at a spot, usually
on its leg, until
the area
becomes a raw,
open sore.

but corticosteroids are the most
common treatment.

AIRBORNE ALLERGIES

An interesting allergy is pollen
allergy. Humans have hay fever, rose
fever and other fevers with which
they suffer during the pollinating
season. Many dogs suffer the same
allergies. When the pollen count is
high, your dog might suffer but
don't expect them to sneeze and
have runny noses like humans. Dogs
react to pollen allergies the same
way they react to fleas—they scratch
and bite themselves. Golden
Retrievers are very susceptible to
airborne pollen allergies.

Dogs, like humans, can be
tested for allergens. Discuss the
testing with your veterinary
dermatologist.

FOOD PROBLEMS
FOOD ALLERGIES
Dogs are allergic to many foods that
are best-sellers and highly
recommended by breeders and
veterinary surgeons. Changing the
brand of food that you buy may not
eliminate the problem if the element
to which the dog is allergic is
contained in the new brand.

Recognising a food allergy is
difficult. Humans vomit or have
rashes when they eat a food to
which they are allergic. Dogs neither
vomit nor (usually) develop a rash.
They react in the same manner as
they do to an
airborne or flea
allergy: they itch,
scratch and

DID YOU KNOW?
You are your dog's caretaker and his
dentist. Vets warn that plaque and
tartar buildup on the teeth will
damage the gums and allow bacteria to
enter the dog's bloodstream, causing
serious damage to the animal's vital
organs. Studies show that over 50
percent of dogs have some form of
gum disease before age three. Daily or
weekly tooth cleaning (with a brush or
soft gauze pad wipes) can add years to
your dog's life.

bite. Thus making the diagnosis extremely difficult. Whilst pollen allergies and parasite bites are usually seasonal, food allergies are year-round problems.

FOOD INTOLERANCE

Food intolerance is the inability of the dog to completely digest certain foods. Puppies that may have done very well on their mother's milk may not do well on cow's milk. The rest of this food intolerance may be lose bowels, passing gas and stomach pains. These are the only obvious symptoms of food intolerance and that makes diagnosis difficult.

TREATING FOOD PROBLEMS

It is possible to handle food allergies and food intolerance yourself. Put your dog on a diet that it has never had. Obviously if it has never eaten this new food it can't have been allergic or intolerant of it. Start with a single ingredient that is not in the dog's diet at the present time. Ingredients like chopped beef or fish are common in dog's diets, so try something more exotic like ostrich, rabbit, pheasant or even just vegetables. Keep the dog on this

diet (with no additives) for a month. If the symptoms of food allergy or intolerance disappear, chances are your dog has a food allergy.

Don't think that the single ingredient cured the problem. You still must find a suitable diet and ascertain which ingredient in the old diet was objectionable. This is most easily done by adding ingredients to the new diet one at a time. Let the dog stay on the modified diet for a month before you add another ingredient. Eventually, you will determine the ingredient that caused the adverse reaction.

An alternative method is to carefully study the ingredients in the diet to which your dog is allergic or intolerable. Identify the main ingredient in this diet and eliminate the main ingredient by buying a different food that does not have that ingredient. Keep experimenting until the symptoms disappear after one month on the new diet.

A scanning electron micrograph (S. E. M.) of a dog flea, *Ctenocephalides canis*.

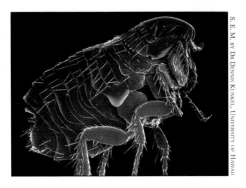

S. E. M. BY DR DENNIS KUNKEL, UNIVERSITY OF HAWAII

(Facing Page) A scanning electron micrograph of a dog or cat flea, *Ctenocephalides*, magnified more than 100x. This has been colourised for effect.

EXTERNAL PARASITES

Of all the problems to which dogs are prone, none is more well known and frustrating than fleas. Fleas, as well as ticks and mites, are difficult to prevent but relatively simple to cure. Parasites that are

Magnified head of a dog flea, *Ctenocephalides canis*.

DID YOU KNOW?

Fleas have been around for millions of years and have adapted to changing host animals.

They are able to go through a complete life cycle in less than one month or they can extend their lives to almost two years by remaining as pupae or cocoons. They do not need blood or any other food for up to 20 months.

They have been measured as being able to jump 300,000 times and can jump 150 times their length in any direction including straight up. Those are just a few of the reasons they are so successful in infesting a dog!

harboured inside the body are more difficult to cure but they are easier to control.

FLEAS

To control a flea infestation you have to understand the life cycle of a typical flea. Fleas are basically a summertime problem and their effective treatment (destruction) is environmental. There is no single flea-control medicine (insecticide) that can be used in every flea-infested area. To understand flea control you must apply suitable treatment to the weak link in the life cycle of the flea.

THE LIFE CYCLE OF A FLEA

Fleas are found in four forms: eggs, larvae, pupae and adults. You really need a low-power microscope or hand lens to identify a living flea's eggs, pupae or larva. They spend

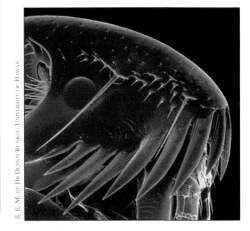

S. E. M. BY DR DENNIS KUNKEL, UNIVERSITY OF HAWAII

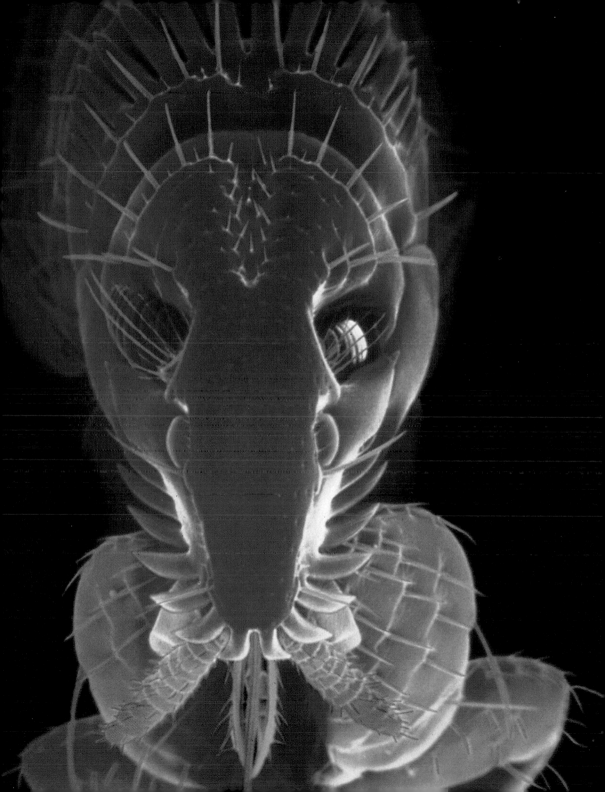

The Life Cycle of the Flea

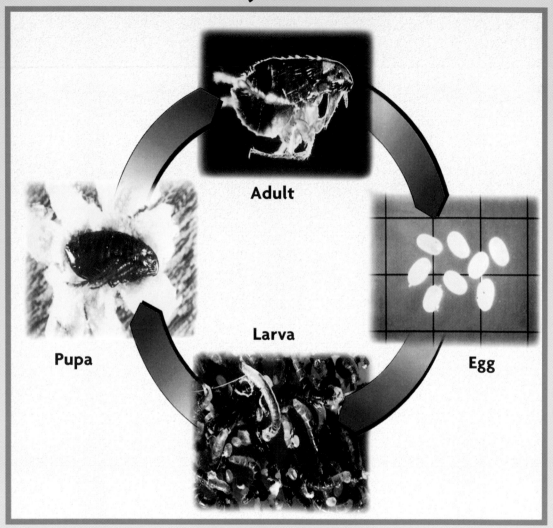

Adult

Pupa

Larva

Egg

The life cycle of the flea was posterised by Fleabusters®. Poster Courtesy of Fleabusters®, R$_x$ for Fleas.

their whole lives on your dog unless they are forcibly removed by brushing, bathing, scratching or biting.

The dog flea is scientifically known as *Ctenocephalides canis* whilst the cat flea is called *Ctenocephalides felis*. Several species infest both dogs and cats.

Fleas lay eggs whilst they are in residence upon your dog. These eggs fall off almost as

Photo by Jean Claude Revy/Phototake

There are many parasiticides which can be used around your home and garden to control fleas.

Natural pyrethrins can be used inside the house.

Allethrin, bioallethrin, permethrin and resmethrin can also be used inside the house but permethrin has been used successfully outdoors, too.

Carbaryl can be used indoors and outdoors.

Propoxur can be used indoors.

Chlorpyrifos, diazinon and malathion can be used indoors or outdoors and it has an extended residual activity.

A male dog flea, *Ctenocephalides canis.*

soon as they dry (they may be a bit damp when initially laid) and are the reservoir of future flea infestations. If your dog scratches himself and is able to dislodge a few fleas, they simply fall off and await a future chance to attack a dog...or even a person. Yes, fleas from dogs bite people. That's why it is so important to control fleas both on the dog and in the dog's entire environment. You must, therefore, treat the dog and the environment simultaneously.

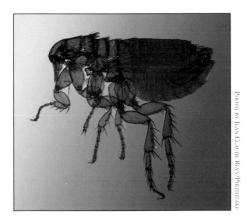

Photo by Jean Claude Revy/Phototake

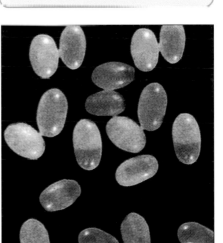

The eggs of the dog flea.

Male cat fleas, *Ctenocephalides felis*, are very commonly found on dogs.

Dwight R Kuhn's magnificent action photo showing a flea jumping from a dog's back.

Photo by Dwight R Kuhn

De-Fleaing the Home
Cleanliness is the simple rule. If you have a cat living with your dog, the matter is more complicated since most dog fleas are actually cat fleas. Cats climb onto many areas that are never accessible to dogs (like window sills, table tops, etc.), so you have to clean all of these areas. The hard floor surfaces (tiles, wood, stone and linoleum) must be mopped several times a day. Drops of food onto the floor are actually food for flea larvae! All rugs and furniture must be vacuumed several times a day. Don't forget closets, under furniture and cushions. A study has reported that a vacuum cleaner with a beater bar can remove only

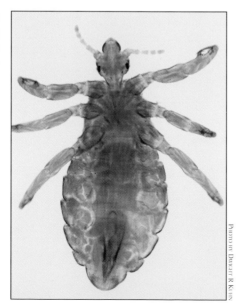

Human lice look like dog lice; the two are closely related.

Photo by Dwight R Kuhn

DID YOU KNOW?
Ivermectin is quickly becoming the drug of choice for treating many parasitic skin diseases in dogs.

For some unknown reason, herding dogs like Collies, Old English Sheepdogs and German Shepherds, etc., are extremely sensitive to ivermectin.

Ivermectin injections have killed some dogs, but dogs heavily infected with skin disorders may be treated anyway.

The ivermectin reaction is a toxicosis that causes tremors, loss of power to move their muscles, prolonged dilatation of the pupil of the eye, coma (unconsciousness), or cessation of breathing (death).

The toxicosis usually starts from 4-6 hours after ingestion (not injection), but can begin as late as 12 hours. The longer it takes to set in, the milder is the reaction.

Ivermectin should only be prescribed and administered by a vet.

Some ivermectin treatments require two doses.

20 percent of the larvae and 50 percent of the eggs. The vacuum bags should be discarded into a sealed plastic bag or burned. The vacuum machine itself should be cleaned. The outdoor area to which your dog has access must also be treated with an insecticide.

Your vet will be able to recommend a household insecticidal spray, but this must be used with caution and instructions strictly adhered to.

There are many drugs available to kill fleas on the dog itself, such as the miracle drug ivermectin, and it is best to have the de-fleaing and de-worming supervised by your vet. Ivermectin is effective against many external and internal parasites including heartworms, roundworms, tapeworms, flukes, ticks and mites. It has not been approved for use to control these pests, but veterinary surgeons frequently use it anyway. Ivermectin may not be available in all areas.

STERILISING THE ENVIRONMENT
Besides cleaning your home with vacuum cleaners and mops, you have to treat the outdoor range of your dog. When trimming bushes and spreading insecticide, be careful not to poison areas in which fishes or other animals reside. Remember to choose dog-safe insecticides, but to be absolutely sure, keep your dog away from treated areas.

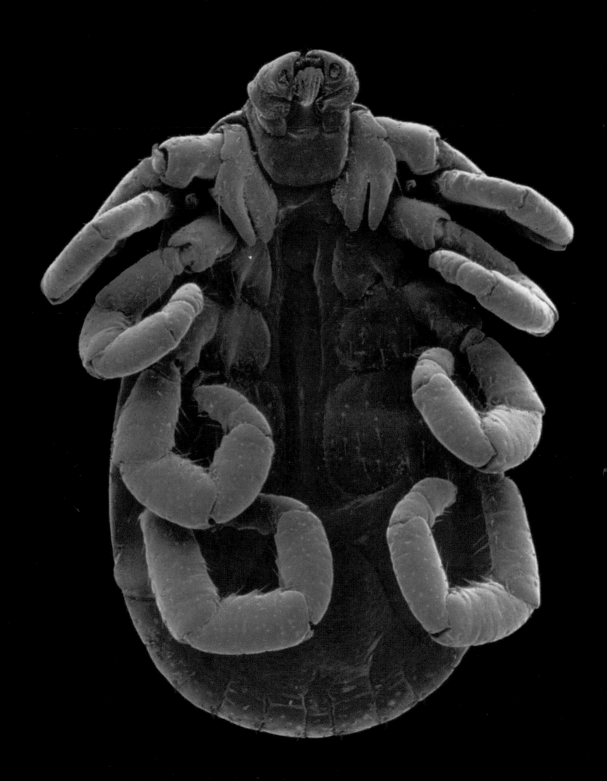

TICKS AND MITES

Though not as common as fleas, ticks and mites are found all over the tropical and temperate world. They don't bite like fleas, they harpoon. They dig their sharp proboscis (nose) into the dog's skin and drink the blood, which is their only food and drink. Dogs can get paralysis, Lyme disease, Rocky Mountain spotted fever (normally found in the U.S.A. only), and many other diseases from ticks and mites. They may live where fleas are found but they also like to hide in cracks or seams in walls wherever dogs live. They are controlled the same way fleas are controlled.

The tick *Dermacentor variabilis* may well be the most common dog tick in many geographical areas, especially where the climate is hot and humid.

Most dog ticks have life expectancies of a week to six months, depending upon climatic conditions. They neither jump nor fly, but crawl slowly and can range up to 5 metres 16 feet) to reach a sleeping or unsuspecting dog.

MANGE

Mange is a skin irritation caused by mites. Some mites are

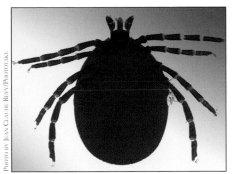

An uncommon dog tick of the genus *Ixode*. Magnified 10x.

contagious, like *Cheyletiella*, ear mites, scabies and chiggers. The non-contagious mites are *Demodex*. The most serious of the mites is the one that causes ear-mite infestation. Ear mites are usually controlled with ivermectin.

It is essential that your dog be treated for mange as quickly as possible because some forms of mange are transmissible to people.

(Facing Page) The dog tick, *Dermacentor variabilis*, is probably the most common tick found on dogs. Look at the strength in its eight legs! No wonder it's hard to detach them.

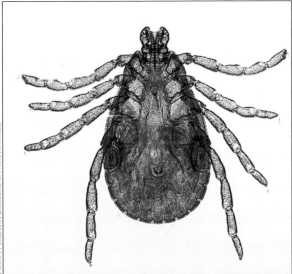

A brown dog tick, *Rhipicephalus sanguineus*, is an uncommon but annoying tick found on dogs.

123

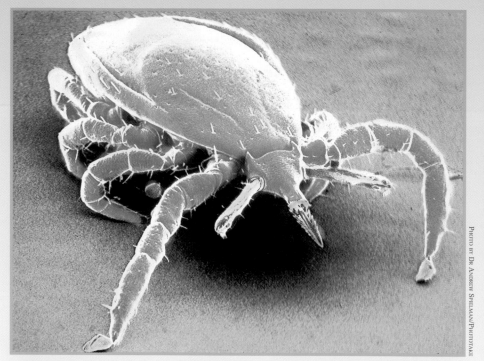

A deer tick, the carrier of Lyme disease.

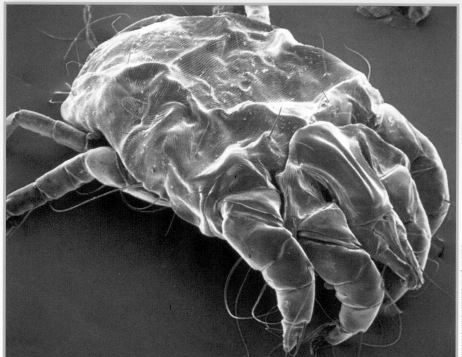

Magnified view of the mange mite, *Psoroptes bovis.*

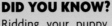

INTERNAL PARASITES

Most animals—fishes, birds and mammals, including dogs and humans—have worms and other parasites that live inside their bodies. According to Dr Herbert R Axelrod, the fish pathologist, there are two kinds of parasites: dumb and smart. The smart parasites live in peaceful coopera-tion with their hosts (symbiosis), whilst the dumb parasites kill their host. Most of the worm infections are relatively easy to control. If they are not controlled they eventually weaken the host dog to the point that other medical problems occur, but they are not dumb parasites that direct-ly cause the death of their hosts.

ROUNDWORMS

The roundworms that infect dogs are scientifically known as *Toxocara canis.* They live in the dog's intestine and shed eggs continually. It has been estimated that an average-sized dog produces about 150 grammes of faeces every day. Each gramme of faeces averages 10,000–12,000 eggs of round-worms. All areas in which dogs

DID YOU KNOW?

Ridding your puppy of worms is VERY IMPORTANT because certain worms that puppies carry, such as tapeworms and roundworms, can infect humans.

Breeders initiate a deworming programme at or about four weeks of age. The routine is repeated every two or three weeks until the puppy is three months old. The breeder from whom you obtained your puppy should provide you with the complete details of the deworming programme.

Your veterinary surgeon can prescribe and monitor the programme of deworming for you. The usual programme is treating the puppy every 15 to 20 days until the puppy is positively worm free.

It is not advised that you treat your puppy with drugs that are not recommended professionally.

The roundworm can infect both dogs and humans.

PHOTO BY CAROLINA BIOLOGICAL SUPPLY/PHOTOTAKE.

125

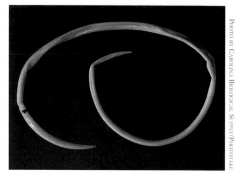

The roundworm *Rhabditis*.

Photo by Carolina Biological Supply/Phototake

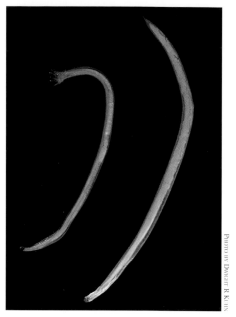

Photo by Dwight R Kuhn

Male and female hookworms, *Ancylostoma caninum*, are uncommonly found in pet or show dogs in Britain. Hookworms may infect other dogs that have exposure to grasslands.

roam contain astronomical numbers of roundworm eggs. The greatest danger of roundworms is that they infect people, too! It is wise to have your dog tested regularly for roundworms.

Pigs also have roundworm infections that can be passed to human and dogs. The typical pig roundworm parasite is called *Ascaris lumbricoides*.

HOOKWORMS

The worm *Ancylostoma caninum* is commonly called the dog hookworm. It is also dangerous to humans and cats. It attaches itself to the dog's intestines by its teeth. It changes the site of its attachment about six times a day, and the dog loses blood from each detachment. This blood loss can cause iron-deficiency anaemia. Hookworms are easily purged from the dog with many medications, the best of which seems to be ivermectin even though it has not been approved for such use.

TAPEWORMS

There are many species of tapeworms, many of which are carried by fleas! The dog eats the flea and starts the tapeworm cycle. Humans can also be infected with tapeworms, so don't eat fleas! Fleas are so small that your dog could pass them onto your

DID YOU KNOW?

Caring for the puppy starts before the puppy is born by keeping the dam healthy and well-nourished. Most puppies have worms, even if they are not evident, so a worming programme is essential. The worms continually shed eggs except during their dormant stage, when they just rest in the tissues of the puppy. During this stage they are not evident during a routine examination.

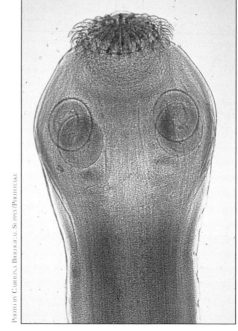

The infective stage of the hookworm larva.

PHOTO BY G. JAMES WEBB/PHOTOTAKE

hands, your plate or your food and make it possible for you to ingest a flea which is carrying tapeworm eggs.

Whilst tapeworm infection is not life threatening in dogs (smart parasite!), it can be the cause of a very serious liver disease for humans. About 50 percent of the humans infected with *Echinococcus multilocularis*, causing alveolar hydatis, perish.

The head and rostellum (the round prominence on the scolex) of a tapeworm, which infects dogs and humans.

PHOTO BY CAROLINA BIOLOGICAL SUPPLY/PHOTOTAKE

HEARTWORMS

Heartworms are thin, extended worms up to 30 cms (12 ins) long that live in a dog's heart and the major blood vessels around it. Your pet may have up to 200 of these worms. The symptoms may

DID YOU KNOW?

Humans, rats, squirrels, foxes, coyotes, wolves, mixed breeds of dogs and purebred dogs are all susceptible to tapeworm infection. Except in humans, tapeworms are usually not a fatal infection. Infected individuals can harbour a thousand parasitic worms. Tapeworms have two sexes— male and female (many other worms have only one sex—male and female in the same worm). If dogs eat infected rats or mice, they get the tapeworm disease.

One month after attaching to a dog's intestine, the worm starts shedding eggs. These eggs are infective immediately. Infective eggs can live for a few months without a host animal. Roundworms, whipworms and tapeworms are just a few of the other commonly known worms that infect dogs.

be loss of energy, loss of appetite, coughing, the development of a pot belly and anaemia.

Heartworms are transmitted by mosquitoes. The mosquito drinks the blood of an infected dog and takes in larvae with the blood. The larvae, called microfilaria, develop within the body of the mosquito and are passed on to the next dog bitten after the larvae mature. It takes two to three weeks for the larvae to develop to the infective stage within the body of the mosquito. Dogs should be treated at about six weeks of age, then every six months.

Blood testing for heartworms is not necessarily indicative of how seriously your dog is infected. This is a dangerous disease. Dogs in the United Kingdom are not affected by heartworm.

The heartworm, *Dirofilaria immitis.*

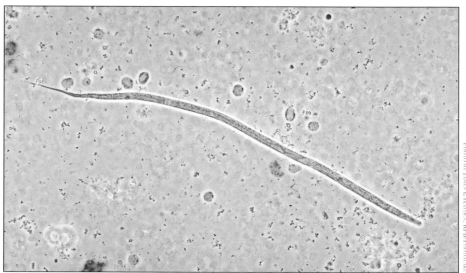

PHOTO BY JAMES E. HAYDEN, RPB/PHOTOTAKE

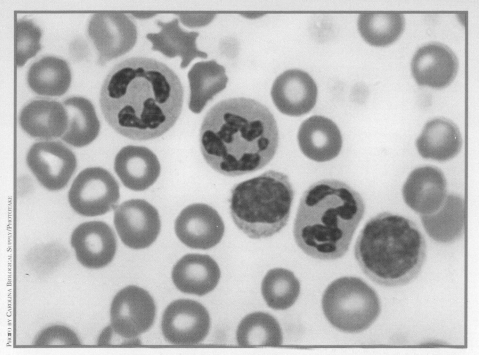

Magnified
heartworm
larvae,
*Dirofilaria
immitis.*

The heart
of a dog infected
with canine
heartworm,
*Dirofilaria
immitis.*

HEALTH CONSIDERATIONS IN THE GOLDEN RETRIEVER

It is an unfortunate dog fact that as a breed becomes more popular, health problems increase proportionately. Sadly, Goldens are no exception. While some genetic disorders are common to most

means abnormal or poor development of the hip joint. It occurs most commonly in large breeds of dogs and is known to be inherited. A severe case can render a hunting dog worthless in the field, and even a mild case can cause painful arthritis in the

Compare the two hip joints and you'll understand dysplasia. Hip dysplasia is a badly worn hip joint caused by improper fit of the bone into the socket. It is easily the most common hip problem in Golden Retrievers. Hip dysplasia can only be positively diagnosed by X-ray. Golden Retrievers manifest the problem when they are between four and nine months of age, the so-called fast growth period.

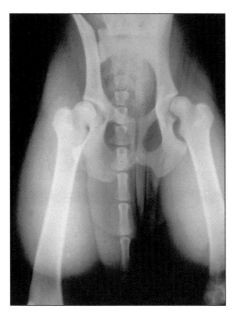
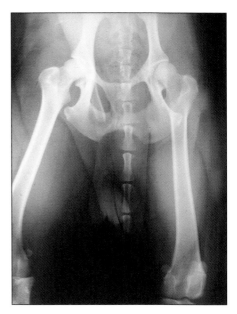

large sporting breeds, others have become more prevalent in Goldens in recent years. Hereditary disease can make life difficult or painful for the afflicted animal, and it might, in some cases, be fatal for the dog.

HIP DYSPLASIA
Simply stated, hip dysplasia

average house dog. Diagnosed only through X-ray examination, less severe cases may go undetected until the dog's ability becomes impaired.

While hip dysplasia is largely an inherited condition, research shows that environmental factors play a significant role in its development. Overfeeding and feeding a diet high in calories (primarily fat) during a puppy's rapid-growth stages are suspected to be contributing factors to the development of HD, and heavy-bodied and overweight puppies are more at risk than pups with very lean conformation.

The British Veterinary Association has joined with The Kennel Club to help curb the incidence of hip dysplasia in all breeds of dogs. Goldens over one year and under six years of age should be X-rayed by a veterinary surgeon. The X-rays are submitted to a special board of veterinary surgeons who specialise in reading orthopaedic films. If the dog shows no evidence of

The healthy hip joint on the right and the unhealthy hip joint on the left.

DO YOU KNOW ABOUT HIP DYSPLASIA?

Hip dysplasia is a fairly common condition found in Golden Retrievers, as well as other breeds. When a dog has hip dysplasia, its hind leg has an incorrectly formed hip joint. By constant use of the hip joint, it becomes more and more loose, wears abnormally and may become arthritic.

Hip dysplasia can only be confirmed with an X-ray, but certain symptoms may indicate a problem. Your Golden Retriever may have a hip dysplasia problem if it walks in a peculiar manner, hops instead of smoothly running, uses his hinds legs in unison (to keep the pressure off the weak joint), has trouble getting up from a prone position and always sits with both legs together on one side of its body.

As the dog matures, it may adapt well to life with a bad hip, but in a few years the arthritis develops and many Golden Retrievers with hip dysplasia become cripples.

Hip dysplasia is considered an inherited disease and can usually be diagnosed when the dog is three to nine months old. Some experts claim that a special diet might help your puppy outgrow the bad hip, but the usual treatments are surgical: the removal of the pectineus muscle, the removal of the round part of the femur, reconstructing the pelvis and replacing the hip with an artificial one. All of these surgical interventions are expensive, but they are usually very successful. Follow the advice of your veterinary surgeon.

Elbow dysplasia in a three-and-a-half-year-old male Golden Retriever.

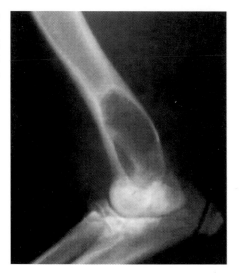

abnormality, a certificate of clearance is issued by The Kennel Club. To correctly identify the dog under evaluation, The Kennel Club requires the dog's date of birth and Kennel Club registration number to be recorded on the X-ray. The purpose of such screening is to eliminate affected dogs from breeding programmes with the long-term goal of reducing the occurrence of hip dysplasia in affected breeds.

Goldens who show marked evidence of hip dysplasia should never be bred. Anyone looking for a healthy Golden puppy should make certain the sire and dam of any litter under consideration have their certificates of clearance.

ELBOW DYSPLASIA (ED) AND OSTEOCHONDROSIS (OCD)

Similar to hip dysplasia, elbow disease is a structural problem of the joints which causes front end lameness in some large breeds of dogs. The symptoms most often appear in the growing dog, usually occurring between four and eight months of age and range from mild to severe. Diagnosis is by X-ray examination, and affected dogs should not be used for breeding purposes.

CATARACTS

A cataract is an opacity of the lens of the eye that has been found to be hereditary in the Golden Retriever. Whilst some cataracts do not interfere with a dog's vision, others can progress into complete or partial blindness. Fortunately today surgery is available to correct some types of cataracts.

Cataracts can be diagnosed by a veterinary ophthalmologic examination as early as six months of age. Eyes should be examined annually until at least three years of age as cataracts can occur later in the dog's life. All Goldens should be cleared before breeding, and affected animals should not be bred.

PROGRESSIVE RETINAL ATROPHY AND RETINAL DYSPLASIA

PRA and RD are inherited defects of the retina (or light receptor area of the eye). They can be diagnosed only by a veterinary surgeon through ophthalmologic examination.

Unlike the progressive deterioration of PRA, RD does not result in total blindness, but will affect a working dog's ability to function at a chosen task. Dogs afflicted with either condition should be removed from breeding programmes.

An owner wishing to certify his dog as free from hereditary cataracts and PRA must be referred to a referee by the examining veterinary surgeon. The referee will examine the dog and review the veterinarian transfer certificate as well as the dog's Kennel Club registration certificate. The referee signs his report, gives one copy to the owner, sends a copy to the British Veterinary Association and keeps one copy for

Your Golden Retriever's eyes should be clear and bright. Any cloudiness or opacity on the lens could indicate a potential problem.

himself. If the report is favourable, The Kennel Club will then issue a permanent or interim certificate of clearance.

EPILEPSY

Epilepsy is a seizure disorder caused by abnormal electrical patterns in the brain. It affects almost all breeds and mixed breeds, although a higher incidence is found in Golden Retrievers and several other breeds.

Primary epilepsy, also known as idiopathic, genetic, inherited or true epilepsy, is difficult to diagnose and there is no specific test for the disease. Ruling out other possibilities generally makes diagnosis. Primary epilepsy usually occurs between the ages of six months and five years of age.

DID YOU KNOW?

There is a 1:4 chance of a puppy getting this fatal gene combination from two parents with recessive genes for acrodermatitis:

AA= NORMAL, HEALTHY
aa= FATAL
Aa= RECESSIVE, NORMAL APPEARING

If the female parent has an Aa gene and the male parent has an Aa gene, the chances are one in four that the puppy will have the fatal genetic combination aa.

		Dam ♀	
		A	a
Sire	A	AA	Aa
	a	Aa	aa

♂

Secondary epilepsy refers to seizures caused by viral or infectious disease, metabolic disorders, chemical or nutritional imbalance or traumatic injury. Seizures are also associated with hypothyroidism, which is an inherited autoimmune disease common to many purebred dogs.

Although epilepsy is difficult to diagnose, dogs suffering recurring seizures, especially from an early age, are questionable breeding candidates.

DID YOU KNOW?

Vaccines do not work all the time. Sometimes dogs are allergic to them and many times the antibodies, which are supposed to be stimulated by the vaccine, just are not produced. You should keep your dog in the veterinary clinic for an hour after it is vaccinated to be sure there are no allergic reactions.

MEDICAL PROBLEMS SEEN IN
GOLDEN RETRIEVERS

Condition	Age Affected	Cause	Area Affected
Acral Lick Dermatitis	Any age, males	Unknown	Legs
Cataracts	6 mos to 3 years	Congenital	Eye
Cleft Palate/Harelip	Newborns	Congenital	Hard or soft palate
Elbow Dysplasia	4 to 7 mos.	Congenital	Elbow joint
Epilepsy	6 mos. to 5 years	Congenital or other	Brain
Gastric Dilatation (Bloat)	Older dogs	Swallowing air	Stomach
Hip Dysplasia	4 to 9 mos.	Congenital	Hip joint
Patellar Luxation	Any age	Congenital or acquired	Kneecaps
Progressive Retinal Atrophy	Older dogs	Congenital	Retina
Retinal Dysplasia	Older dogs	Congenital	Eye
Urolithiasis	Adult	Cystine uroliths/stones	Kidney/Bladder
Von Willebrand's Disease	Birth	Congenital	Blood

Golden Retriever

The term old is a qualitative term. For dogs, as well as their masters, old is relative. Certainly we can all distinguish between a puppy Golden Retriever and an adult Golden Retriever—there are the obvious physical traits, such as size, appearance and facial expressions, and personality traits. Puppies that are nasty are very rare. Puppies and young dogs like to play with children. Children's natural exuberance is a good match for the seemingly endless energy of young dogs. They like to run, jump, chase and retrieve. When dogs grow up and cease their interaction with children, they are often thought of as being too old to play with the kids.

Don't expect your Golden Retriever to act young forever. A Golden in his 'golden' years requires special love and attention from his family.

On the other hand, if a Golden Retriever is only exposed to people over 60 years of age, its life will normally be less active and it will not seem to be getting old as its activity level slows down.

If people live to be 100 years old, dogs live to be 20 years old. Whilst this is a good rule of thumb, it is very inaccurate.

When trying to compare dog years to human years, you cannot make a generalisation about all dogs. You can make the generalisation that, 11 or 12 years is a good life span for a Golden Retriever,

> **DID YOU KNOW?**
> The bottom line is simply that a dog is getting old when YOU think it is getting old because it slows down in its general activities, including walking, running, eating, jumping and retrieving. On the other hand, certain activities increase, like more sleeping, more barking and more repetition of habits like going to the door when you put your coat on without being called.

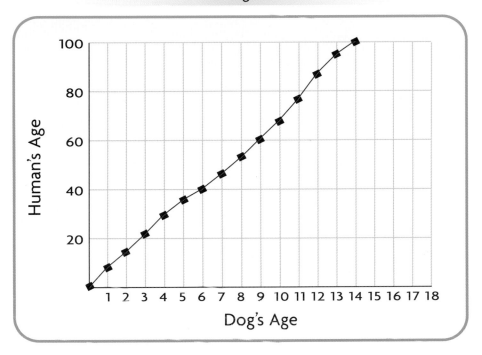

Human's Age (y-axis): 20, 40, 60, 80, 100

Dog's Age (x-axis): 1 2 3 4 5 6 7 8 9 10 11 12 13 14 15 16 17 18

which is quite good compared to many other purebred dogs that may only live to 8 or 9 years of age. Some Golden Retrievers have been known to live to 15 years. Dogs are generally considered mature within three years, but they can reproduce even earlier. So the first three years of a dog's life are like seven times that of comparable humans. That means a 3-year-old dog is like a 21-year-old human. As the curve of comparison shows, there is no hard and fast rule for comparing dog and human ages. The comparison is made even more difficult, for not all humans age at the same rate...and human females live longer than human males.

DID YOU KNOW?

An old dog starts to show one or more of the following symptoms:

• The hair on its face and paws starts to turn grey. The colour breakdown usually starts around the eyes and mouth.

• Sleep patterns are deeper and longer and the old dog is harder to awaken.

• Food intake diminishes.

• Responses to calls, whistles and other signals are ignored more and more.

• Eye contacts do not evoke tail wagging (assuming they once did).

WHAT TO LOOK FOR IN SENIORS

Most veterinary surgeons and behaviourists use the seventh year mark as the time to consider a dog a 'senior.' The term 'senior' does not imply that the dog is geriatric and has begun to fail in mind and body. Ageing is essentially a slowing process. Humans readily admit that they feel a difference in their activity level from age 20 to 30, and then from 30 to 40, etc. By treating the seven-year-old dog

DID YOU KNOW?

The symptoms listed below are symptoms that gradually appear and become more noticeable. They are not life threatening, however, the symptoms below are to be taken very seriously and a discussion with your veterinary surgeon is warranted:

• Your dog cries and whimpers when it moves and stops running completely.

• Convulsions start or become more serious and frequent. The usual convulsion (spasm) is when the dog stiffens and starts to tremble being unable or unwilling to move. The seizure usually lasts for 5 to 30 minutes.

• Your dog drinks more water and urinates more frequently. Wetting and bowel accidents take place indoors without warning.

• Vomiting becomes more and more frequent.

DID YOU KNOW?

Euthanasia must be done by a licensed veterinary surgeon. There also may be societies for the prevention of cruelty to animals in your area. They often offer this service upon a vet's recommendation.

as a senior, owners are able to implement certain therapeutic and preventive medical strategies with the help of their veterinary surgeons. A senior-care programme should include at least two veterinary visits per year, screening sessions to determine the dog's health status, as well as nutritional counselling. Veterinary surgeons determine the senior dog's health status through a blood smear for a complete blood count, serum chemistry profile with electrolytes, urinalysis, blood pressure check, electrocardiogram, ocular tonometry (pressure on the eyeball), and dental prophylaxis.

Such an extensive programme for senior dogs is well advised before owners start to see the obvious physical signs of ageing, such as slower and inhibited movement, greying, increased sleep/nap periods, and disinterest in play and other activity. This preventative programme promises a longer, healthier life for the ageing dog. Amongst the physical problems common in ageing dogs

What the Owner Can Look For

IF YOU NOTICE...	IT COULD INDICATE...
Discolouration of teeth and gums, foul breath, loss of appetite	Abcesses, gum disease, mouth lesions
Lumps, bumps, cysts, warts, fatty tumours	Cancers
Cloudiness of eyes, apparent loss of sight	Cataracts, lenticular sclerosis, PRA, retinal dysplasia, blindness
Flaky coat, alopaecia (hair loss)	Hormonal problems, hypothyroidism
Obesity, appetite loss, excessive weight gain	Various problems
Household accidents, increased urination	Diabetes, kidney or bladder disease
Increased thirst	Kidney disease, diabetes mellitus
Change in sleeping habits, coughing	Heart disease
Difficulty moving	Arthritis, degenerative joint disease, spondylosis (degenerative spine disease)

If the owner notices any of these signs, an appointment should be made immediately with the veterinary surgeon for a thorough evaluation.

are the loss of sight and hearing, arthritis, kidney and liver failure, diabetes mellitus, heart disease, and Cushing's disease (a hormonal disease).

In addition to the physical manifestations discussed, there are some behavioural changes and problems related to ageing dogs. Dogs suffering from hearing or vision loss, dental discomfort or arthritis can become aggressive. Likewise the near-deaf and/or blind dog may be startled more easily and react in an unexpectedly aggressive manner. Seniors suffering from senility can become more impatient and irritable. Housesoiling accidents are associated with loss of mobility, kidney problems, loss of sphincter control as well as plaque accumulation, physiological brain changes, and reactions to medications. Older dogs, just like young puppies, suffer from separation anxiety, which can lead to excessive barking, whining, housesoiling, and destructive behaviour. Seniors may become fearful of everyday sounds, such as vacuum cleaners, heaters, thunder, and passing traffic. Some dogs have difficulty sleeping, due to discomfort, the need for frequent potty visits, and the like. Owners should avoid spoiling the older dog with too many fatty treats. Obesity is a common problem in older dogs and subtracts years from their lifespan. Keep the senior dog as trim as possible since excessive weight puts additional stress on the body's vital organs. Some breeders recommend supplementing the diet with foods high in fibre and lower in calories. Adding fresh vegetables and marrow broth to the senior's diet makes a tasty, low-calorie, low-fat supplement. Vets also offer specialty diets for senior dogs that are worth exploring.

DID YOU KNOW?

Your senior dog may lose interest in eating, not because he's less hungry but because his senses of smell and taste have diminished. The old chow simply does not smell as good as it once did. Additionally, older dogs use less energy and thereby can sustain themselves on less food.

Your dog, as he nears his twilight years, needs his owner's patience and good care more than ever. Never punish an older dog for an accident or abnormal behaviour. For all the years of love, protection and companionship that your dog has provided, he deserves special attention and courtesies. The older dog may need to relieve himself at 3 a.m. because he can no longer hold it for eight hours. Older dogs may not be able to remain crated for more than two or three hours. It may be time to give up a sofa or chair to your old friend. Although he may not seem as enthusiastic about your attention and petting, he does appreciate the considerations you offer as he gets older.

Your Golden Retriever does not understand why his world is slowing down. Owners must make the transition into the golden years as pleasant and rewarding as possible.

WHAT TO DO WHEN THE TIME COMES

You are never fully prepared to make a rational decision about putting your dog to sleep. It is very obvious that you love your Golden Retriever or you would not be reading this book. Putting a loved dog to sleep is extremely difficult. It is a decision that must be made with your veterinary surgeon. You are usually forced to make the decision when one of the life-threatening symptoms listed above becomes serious enough for you to seek medical (veterinary) help.

If the prognosis of the malady indicates the end is near and your beloved pet will only suffer more and experience no enjoyment for the balance of its life, then euthanasia is the right choice.

What is Euthanasia?

Euthanasia derives from the Greek meaning 'good death.' In other words, it means the planned, painless killing of a dog suffering from a painful, incurable condition, or who is so aged that it cannot walk, see, eat or control its excretory functions.

Euthanasia is usually accomplished by injection with an overdose of an anaesthesia or barbiturate. Aside from the prick of the needle, the experience is painless.

How About You?

The decision to euthanize your dog is never easy. The days during which the dog becomes ill and the end occurs can be unusually stressful for you. If this is your first experience with the death of a loved one, you may need the comfort dictated by your religious beliefs. If you are the head of the family and have children, you should have involved them in the decision of putting your Golden Retriever to sleep. Usually your dog can be maintained on drugs for a few days whilst it is kept in the clinic in order to give you ample time to make a decision. During this time, talking with members of the family or religious representatives, or even people who have lived through this same experience, can ease the burden of your inevitable decision. In any case, euthanasia is painful and stressful for the family of the dog. Unfortunately, it does not end there.

The Final Resting Place

Dogs can have the same privileges as humans. They can be buried in a pet cemetery in a burial container (very expensive); buried in your garden in a place suitably marked with a stone, newly planted tree or bush; cremated with the ashes being given to you, or even stuffed and mounted by a taxidermist.

All of these options should be discussed frankly and openly with your veterinary surgeon. Do not be afraid to ask financial questions. Cremations are usually mass burnings and the ashes you get may not be only the ashes of your beloved dog. If you want a

Golden Retriever? Perhaps you want a smaller or larger dog? How much do you want to spend on a dog? Look in your local newspapers for advertisements (DOGS FOR SALE), or, better yet, consult your local society for the prevention of cruelty to animals to adopt a dog. It is harder to find puppies at an animal shelter, but there are often many adult dogs in need of new homes. You may be able to find another Golden Retriever, or you may choose another breed or a mixed-breed dog. Private breeders are the best source for high-quality puppies and dogs.

Whatever you decide, do it as quickly as possible. Most people usually buy the same breed because they know (and love) the characteristics of that breed. Then, too, they often know people who have the same breed and perhaps they are lucky enough that one of their friends expects a litter soon. What could be better?

private cremation, there are small crematoriums available to all veterinary clinics. Your vet can usually arrange for this but it may be a little more expensive.

Cemeteries for pets exist and they sometimes have special depositories for the ashes of your beloved pet.

GETTING ANOTHER DOG?

The grief of losing your beloved dog will be as lasting as the grief of losing a human friend or relative. You cannot go out and buy another grandfather, but you can go out and buy another Golden Retriever. In most cases, if your dog died of old age (if there is such a thing), it had slowed down considerably. Do you want a new Golden Retriever puppy to replace it? Or are you better off in finding a more mature Golden Retriever, say two to three years of age, which will usually be housetrained and will have an already developed personality. In this case, you can find out if you like each other after a few hours of being together.

The decision is, of course, your own. Do you want another

CDS: COGNITIVE DYSFUNCTION SYNDROME
"Old Dog Syndrome"

There are many ways to evaluate old-dog syndrome. Veterinary surgeons have defined CDS (cognitive dysfunction syndrome) as the gradual deterioration of cognitive abilities. These are indicated by changes in the dog's behaviour. When a dog changes its routine response, and maladies have been eliminated as the cause of these behavioural changes, then CDS is the usual diagnosis.

More than half the dogs over 8 years old suffer some form of CDS. The older the dog, the more chance it has of suffering from CDS. In humans, doctors often dismiss the CDS behavioural changes as part of 'winding down.'

There are four major signs of CDS: frequent toilet accidents inside the home, sleeps much more or much less than normal, acts confused, and fails to respond to social stimuli.

SYMPTOMS OF CDS

FREQUENT TOILET ACCIDENTS
- *Urinates in the house.*
- *Defecates in the house.*
- *Doesn't signal that he wants to go out.*

SLEEP PATTERNS
- *Moves much more slowly.*
- *Sleeps more than normal during the day.*
- *Sleeps less during the night.*
- *Walks around listlessly and without a destination goal.*

CONFUSION
- *Goes outside and just stands there.*
- *Appears confused with a faraway look in his eyes.*
- *Hides more often.*
- *Doesn't recognise friends.*
- *Doesn't come when called.*

FAILS TO RESPOND TO SOCIAL STIMULI
- *Comes to people less frequently, whether called or not.*
- *Doesn't tolerate petting for more than a short time.*
- *Doesn't come to the door when you return home from work.*

UNDERSTANDING THE BEHAVIOUR OF YOUR
Golden Retriever

As a Golden Retriever owner, you have selected your dog so that you and your loved ones can have a companion, a protector, a friend and a four-legged family member. You invest time, money and effort to care for and train the family's new charge. Of course, this chosen canine behaves perfectly! Well, perfectly like a dog.

THINK LIKE A DOG

Dogs do not think like humans, nor do humans think like dogs, though we try. Unfortunately, a dog is incapable of figuring out how humans think, so the responsibility falls on the owner to adopt a proper canine mindset. Dogs cannot rationalise, and dogs exist in the present moment. Many dog owners make the mistake in training of thinking

DID YOU KNOW?

Punishment is rarely necessary for a misbehaving dog. Dogs that are habitually bad probably had a poor education and they do not know what is expected of them. They need training. Disciplinary behaviour on your part usually does more harm than good.

that they can reprimand their dog for something he did a while ago. Basically, you cannot even reprimand a dog for something he did 20 seconds ago! Either catch him in the act or forget it! It is a waste of your and your dog's time—in his mind, you are

reprimanding him for whatever he is doing at that moment.

The following behavioural problems represent some which owners most commonly encounter. Every dog is unique and every situation is unique. No author could purport to solve your Golden Retriever's problem simply by reading a script. Here we outline some basic 'dogspeak' so that owners' chances of solving behavioural problems are increased. Discuss bad habits with your veterinary surgeon and he/she can recommend a behavioural specialist to consult in appropriate cases. Since behavioural abnormalities are the leading reason owners abandon their pets, we hope that you will make a valiant effort to solve your Golden Retriever's problem. Patience and understanding are virtues that dwell in every pet-loving household.

Golden Retriever puppies learn manners from their dams. Licking the neck of the dam indicates the subordination of the pup to the pack leader.

> **DID YOU KNOW?**
> Physical games like pulling contests, wrestling, jumping and teasing should not be encouraged. Inciting the dog's crazy behaviour tends to confuse a dog. The owner has to be able to control his dog at all times; even in play, your dog has to know you're the leader and you decide when to play and when to behave mannerly.

AGGRESSION

Although nobody considers the Golden Retriever to be a mean or vicious breed, aggression is always a concern among dog owners. Goldens are not naturally aggressive, but aggressive tendencies can show up in dogs of any breed for a number of reasons.

Aggression, when not controlled, always becomes dangerous. An aggressive dog, no matter the size, may lunge at, bite or even attack a person or another dog. Aggressive behaviour is not to be tolerated. It is more than just inappropriate behaviour; it is not

safe. It is painful for a family to watch their dog become unpredictable in his behaviour to the point where they are afraid of him. Whilst not all aggressive behaviour is dangerous, growling, baring teeth, etc., can be frightening: It is important to ascertain why the dog is acting in this manner. Aggression is a display of dominance, and the dog should not have the dominant role in its pack, which is, in this case, your family.

It is important not to challenge an aggressive dog as this could provoke an attack. Observe your Golden Retriever's body language. Does he make direct eye contact and stare? Does he try to make himself as large as

The posture of a strange dog can tell you whether he's being friendly or threatening. Most Goldens are non-aggressive and approachable.

possible: head up, chest out, tail erect? Height and size signify authority in a dog pack—being taller or 'above' another dog literally means that he is 'above' in the social status. These body signals tell you that your Golden Retriever thinks he is in charge, a problem that needs to be

DID YOU KNOW?

DANGER! If you and your on-lead dog are approached by a larger, running dog that is not restrained, walk away from the dog as quickly as possible. Don't allow your dog to make eye contact with the other dog. You should not make eye contact either. In dog terms, eye contact indicates a challenge.

addressed. An aggressive dog is unpredictable: you never know when he is going to strike and what he is going to do. You cannot understand why a dog that is playful and loving one minute is growling and snapping the next.

The best solution is to consult a behavioural specialist, one who has experience with the Golden Retriever if possible. Together, perhaps you can pinpoint the cause of your dog's aggression and do something about it. An aggressive dog cannot be trusted, and a dog that cannot be trusted is not safe to have as a family pet. If the pet

DID YOU KNOW?

Fear in a grown dog is often the result of improper or incomplete socialisation as a pup, or it can be the result of a traumatic experience he suffered when young. Keep in mind that the term 'traumatic' is relative— something that you would not think twice about can leave a lasting negative impression on a puppy. If the dog experiences a similar experience later in life, he may try to fight back to protect himself. Again, this behaviour is very unpredictable, especially if you do not know what is triggering his fear.

Golden Retriever becomes untrustworthy, he cannot be kept in the home with the family. The family must get rid of the dog. In the worst case, the dog must be euthanized.

AGGRESSION TOWARD OTHER DOGS
In general, a dog's aggressive behaviour toward another dog stems from not enough exposure to other dogs at an early age. If other dogs make your Golden Retriever nervous and agitated, he will lash out as a defensive mechanism. A dog who has not received sufficient exposure to other canines tends to believe that he is the only dog on the planet. The animal becomes so dominant that he does not even show signs that he is fearful or threatened. Without growling or any other physical signal as a warning, he will lunge at and bite the other dog. A way to correct this is to let your Golden Retriever approach another dog when walking on lead. Watch very closely and at the very first sign of aggression, correct your

Golden Retriever and pull him away. Scold him for any sign of discomfort, and then praise him when he ignores or tolerates the other dog. Keep this up until he stops the aggressive behaviour, learns to ignore the other dog or accepts other dogs. Praise him lavishly for his correct behaviour.

Meeting along the trail is enjoyable for the hikers. When introducing your Golden to strange dogs, it's best to keep all dogs on lead in case one dog becomes aggressive.

DOMINANT AGGRESSION
A social hierarchy is firmly established in a wild dog pack. The dog wants to dominate those under him and please those above him. Dogs know that there must

be a leader. If you are not the obvious choice for emperor, the dog will assume the throne! These conflicting innate desires are what a dog owner is up against when he sets about training a dog. In training a dog to obey commands, the owner is reinforcing that he is the top dog in the 'pack' and that the dog should, and should want to, serve his superior. Thus, the owner is suppressing the dog's urge to dominate by modifying his behaviour and making him obedient.

An important part of training is taking every opportunity to reinforce that you are the leader. The simple action of making your Golden Retriever sit to wait for his food says that you control when he eats and that he is dependent on you for food. Although it may be difficult, do not give in to your dog's wishes every time he whines at you or looks at you with his pleading eyes. It is a constant effort to show the dog that his place in the pack is at the bottom. This is not meant to sound cruel or inhumane. You love your Golden Retriever and you should treat him with care and affection. You (hopefully) did not get a dog just so you could boss around another creature. Dog training is not about being cruel or feeling important, it is about moulding the dog's behaviour into what is acceptable and teaching him to live by your rules. In theory, it is

Not usually considered 'pack dogs,' Golden Retrievers generally do very well in large groups. Some owners own a half dozen dogs and allow them to romp and play together constantly.

DID YOU KNOW?

Your dog inherited the pack-leader mentality. He only knows about pecking order. He instinctively wants to be top dog but you have to convince him that you are boss. There is no such thing as living in a democracy with your dog. You are the dictator, the absolute monarch.

quite simple: catch him in appropriate behaviour and reward him for it. Add a dog into the equation and it becomes a bit more trying, but as a rule of thumb, positive reinforcement is what works best.

With a dominant dog, punishment and negative reinforcement can have the opposite effect of what you are after. It can make a dog fearful and/or act out aggressively if he feels he is being challenged. Remember, a dominant dog perceives himself at the top of the social heap and will fight to defend his perceived status. The best way to prevent that is never to give him reason to think that he is in control in the first place. If you are having trouble training your Golden Retriever and it seems as if he is constantly challenging your authority, seek the help of an obedience trainer or behavioural specialist. A professional will work with both you and your dog to teach you effective techniques to use at home. Beware of trainers who rely on excessively harsh methods; scolding is necessary now and then, but the focus in your training should always be on positive reinforcement.

If you can isolate what brings out the fear reaction, you can help the dog get over it. Supervise your Golden Retriever's interactions with people and other dogs, and praise the dog when it goes well. If he starts to act aggressively in a

DID YOU KNOW?

When a dog bites there is always a good reason for it doing so. Many dogs are trained to protect a person, an area or an object When that person, area or object is violated, the dog will attack. A dog attacks with its mouth. It has no other means of attack. It never uses teeth for defense. It merely runs away or lays down on the ground when it is in an indefensible situation. Fighting dogs (and there are many breeds which fight) are taught to fight, but they also have a natural instinct to fight. This instinct is normally reserved for other dogs, though unfortunate accidents occur when babies crawl towards a fighting dog and the dog mistakes the crawling child as a potential attacker.

If a dog is a biter for no reason; if it bites the hand that feeds it; if it snaps at members of your family, see your veterinarian immediately for behavioural modification treatments.

149

situation, correct him and remove him from the situation. Do not let people approach the dog and start petting him without your express permission. That way, you can have the dog sit to accept petting, and praise him when he behaves properly. You are focusing on praise and on modifying his behaviour by rewarding him when he acts appropriately. By being gentle and by supervising

DID YOU KNOW?
We all love our dogs and our dogs love us. They show their love and affection by licking us. This is not a very sanitary

practice as dogs lick and sniff in some unsavory places. Kissing your dog on the mouth is strictly forbidden, as parasites can be transmitted in this manner.

DID YOU KNOW?
Dogs get to know each other by sniffing each other's backsides.

It seems that each dog has a telltale odor probably created by the anal glands. It also distinguishes sex and signals when a female will be receptive to a male's attention.

Some dog's snap at the other dog's intrusion of their private parts.

his interactions, you are showing him that there is no need to be afraid or defensive.

SEXUAL BEHAVIOUR
Dogs exhibit certain sexual behaviours that may have influenced your choice of male or female when you first bought your Golden Retriever. Spaying/neutering will eliminate these behaviours, but if you are purchasing a dog that you wish to breed, you should be aware of what you will have to deal with throughout the dog's life.

Female dogs usually have two oestruses per year with each season lasting about three weeks. These are the only times in which a female dog will mate, and she usually will not allow this until the second week of the cycle. If a bitch is not bred during the heat cycle, it is not uncommon for her to experience a false pregnancy, in which her mammary glands swell and she exhibits maternal tendencies toward toys or other objects.

Owners must further recognise that mounting is not merely a sexual expression but also one of dominance. Be consistent and persistent and you will find that you can 'move mounters.'

CHEWING

The national canine pastime is chewing! Every dog loves to sink his 'canines' into a tasty bone, but sometimes that bone is attached to his owner's hand! Dogs need to chew, to massage their gums, to make their new teeth feel better and to exercise their jaws. This is a natural behaviour deeply imbedded in all things canine. Our role as owners is not to stop chewing, but to redirect it to positive, chew-worthy objects. Be an informed owner and purchase proper chew toys like strong nylon bones made for active dogs like your Golden Retriever. Be sure that the devices are safe and durable, since your dog's safety is at risk. Again, the owner is responsible for ensuring a dog-proof environment. The best answer is prevention: that is, put your shoes, handbags and other tasty objects in their proper places (out of the reach of the growing canine mouth). Direct puppies to their toys whenever you see them tasting the furniture legs or your trouser leg. Make a loud noise to attract the pup's attention and immediately escort him to his chew toy and engage him with the toy for at least four minutes, praising and encouraging him all the while.

Some trainers recommend deterrents, such as hot pepper or another bitter spice or a product designed for this purpose, to discourage the dog from chewing unwanted objects. This is sometimes reliable, though not as often as the manufacturers of such products claim. Test out the product with your own dog before investing in a case of it.

DID YOU KNOW?

Dogs and humans may be the only animals that smile. Dogs imitate the smile on their owner's face when he

greets a friend. The dog only smiles at its human friends. It never smiles at another dog or cat. Usually it rolls up its lips and shows its teeth in a clenched mouth while it rolls over onto its back begging for a soft scratch.

JUMPING UP

Jumping up is a dog's friendly way of saying hello! Some dog owners do not mind when their dog jumps up, which is fine for them. The problem arises when guests come to the house and the dog greets them in the same manner—whether they like it or not! However friendly the greeting may be, chances are your visitors will not appreciate being knocked over by your boisterous Golden Retriever. The dog will not be able to distin-

DID YOU KNOW?

You should never play tug-of-war games with your puppy. Such games create a struggle for 'top dog' position and teach the puppy that it is okay to challenge you. It will also encourage your puppy's natural tendency to bite down hard and *win*.

DID YOU KNOW?

Males, whether castrated or not, will mount almost anything: a pillow, your leg or, much to your horror, even your neighbour's leg. As with other types of inappropriate behaviour, the dog must be corrected while in the act, which for once is not difficult. Often he will not let go! While a puppy is experimenting with his very first urges, his owners feel he needs to 'sow his oats' and allow the pup to mount. As the pup grows into a full-size dog, with full-size urges, it becomes a nuisance and an embarrassment. Males always appear as if they are trying to 'save the race,' more determined and stronger than imaginable. While altering the dog at an appropriate age will limit the dog's desire, it usually does not remove it entirely.

guish upon whom he can jump and whom he cannot. Therefore, it is probably best to discourage this behaviour entirely.

Pick a command such as 'Off.' (avoid using 'Down' since you will use that for the dog to lie down) and tell him 'Off' when he jumps up. Place him on the ground on all fours and have him sit, praising him the whole time. Always lavish him with praise and petting when he is in the sit position. That way you are still giving him a warm affectionate greeting, because you are as excited to see him as he is to see you!

DIGGING

Digging, which is seen as a destructive behaviour to humans, is actually quite a natural behaviour in dogs. Although your Golden Retriever is not one of the 'earth dogs' (also known as terriers), his desire to dig can be irrepressible and most frustrating to his owners. When digging occurs in

DID YOU KNOW?
Stop a dog from jumping before he jumps. If he is getting ready to jump onto you, simply walk away. If he jumps on you before you can turn away, lift your knee so that it bumps him in the chest. Do not be forceful. Your dog will realise that jumping up is not a productive way of getting attention.

your garden, it is actually a normal behaviour redirected into something the dog can do in his everyday life. In the wild, a dog would be actively seeking food, making his own shelter, etc. He would be using his paws in a purposeful manner for his survival. Since you provide him with food and shelter, he has no need to use his paws for these purposes, and so the energy that he would be using manifests itself in the form of little holes all over your garden and flower beds.

Perhaps your dog is digging as a reaction to boredom—it is somewhat similar to someone eating a whole bag of crisps in front of the TV—because they are there and there is not anything better to do! Basically, the answer is to provide the dog with adequate play and exercise so that his mind and paws are occupied, and so that he feels as if he is doing something useful.

Of course, digging is easiest to control if it is stopped as soon as possible, but it is often hard to catch a dog in the act, especially if he is alone in the garden during the day. If your dog is a compulsive digger and is not easily distracted by other activities, you can designate an area on your property where it is okay for him to dig. If you catch him digging in an off-limits area of the garden, immediately bring him to the approved area and praise him for digging there. Keep a close eye on him so that you can catch him in the act—that is the only way to make him understand what is permitted and what is not. If you bring him to a hole he dug an hour

Jumping up is unacceptable behaviour in any dog, especially one as heavy as the Golden Retriever. Although he thinks he's being friendly, jumping up can be dangerous and must be properly handled.

153

ago and tell him 'No,' he will understand that you are not fond of holes, or dirt, or flowers. If you catch him whilst he is stifle-deep in your tulips, that is when he will get your message.

BARKING

Dogs cannot talk—oh, what they would say if they could! Instead, barking is a dog's way of 'talking.' It can be somewhat frustrating because it is not always easy to tell what a dog means by his bark—is he excited, happy, frightened or angry? Whatever it is that the dog is trying to say, he should not be punished for barking. Only when the barking becomes excessive, and when the excessive barking becomes a bad habit, does the behaviour need to be modified.

If an intruder came into your home in the middle of the night

> **DID YOU KNOW?**
> Barking is your dog's way of protecting you. If he barks at a stranger walking past your house, a moving car or a fleeing cat, he is merely exercising his responsibility to protect his pack (YOU) and territory from a perceived intruder. Since the 'intruder' usually keeps going, the dog thinks his barking chased it away and he feels fulfilled. This behaviour leads your overly vocal friend to believe that he is the 'dog in charge.'

and your Golden Retriever barked a warning, wouldn't you be pleased? You would probably deem your dog a hero, a wonderful guardian and protector of the home. However, if a friend drops by unexpectedly and rings the doorbell and is greeted with a sudden sharp bark, you would probably be annoyed at the dog.

There are no limits to the talents of the Golden Retriever. Whilst not many Goldens are employed as sled dogs, this gifted Golden joins his Samoyed housemates to be the exception!

But in reality, isn't this just the same behaviour? The dog does not know any better...unless he sees who is at the door and it is someone he knows, he will bark as a means of vocalising that his (and your) territory is being threatened. Whilst your friend is not posing a threat, it is all the same to the dog. Barking is his means of letting you know that there is an intrusion, whether friend or foe, on your property. This type of barking is instinctive and should not be discouraged.

Excessive habitual barking, however, is a problem that should be corrected early on. As your Golden Retriever grows up, you will be able to tell when his barking is purposeful and when it is for no reason. You will become able to distinguish your dog's different barks and their meanings. For example, the bark when someone comes to the door will be different from the bark when he is excited to see you. It is similar to a person's tone of voice, except that the dog has to rely totally on tone of voice because he does not have the benefit of using words. An incessant barker will be evident at an early age.

There are some things that encourage a dog to bark. For example, if your dog barks non-stop for a few minutes and you give him a treat to quiet him, he believes that you are rewarding him for barking. He will associate barking with getting a treat, and will do it until he is rewarded.

FOOD STEALING

Is your dog devising ways of stealing food from your cupboard? If so, you must answer the following questions: Is your Golden Retriever hungry, or is he 'constantly famished' like every other chow hound? Why is there food on the counter top? Face it, some dogs are more food-motivated than others. Some dogs are totally obsessed by a slab of brisket and can only think of their next meal. Food stealing is terrific fun and always yields a great reward—FOOD, glorious food.

The owner's goal, therefore, is to make the 'reward' less rewarding, even startling! Plant a shaker can (an empty pop can with coins inside) on the counter so that it catches your pooch offguard. There are other devices available that will surprise the dog when he is looking for a mid-afternoon snack. Such remote-control devices, though not the first choice of some trainers, allow the correction to come from the object instead of the owner. These devices are also useful to keep the snacking hound from napping on furniture that is forbidden.

Goldens can become beggars. They will put on their most enchanting face and whine until you share your food with them.

BEGGING

Just like food stealing, begging is a favourite pastime of hungry puppies! It yields that same lovely reward—FOOD! Dogs quickly learn that their

owners keep the 'good food' for themselves, and that we humans do not dine on kibble alone. Begging is a conditioned response related to a specific stimulus, time and place. The sounds of the kitchen, cans

and bottles opening, crinkling bags, the smell of food in preparation, etc., will excite the chow hound and soon the paws are in the air!

Here is the solution to stopping this behaviour: Never give in to a beggar! You are rewarding the dog for sitting pretty, jumping up, whining and rubbing his nose into you by giving him that glorious reward—food. By ignoring the dog, you will (eventually) force the behaviour into extinction. Note that the behaviour likely gets worse before it disappears, so be

> **DID YOU KNOW?**
> Never allow your puppy to growl at you or bare his tiny teeth. Such behaviour is dominant and aggressive. If not corrected, the dog will repeat the behaviour, which will become more threatening as he grows larger and will eventually lead to biting.

Goldens get lonely without almost constant attention from their masters. Owning two Goldens can reduce the stress of separation anxiety, though the dogs will still keenly anticipate your return home.

sure there are not any 'softies' in the family who will give in to little 'Oliver' every time he whimpers, 'More, please.'

SEPARATION ANXIETY
Your Golden Retriever may howl, whine or otherwise vocalise his displeasure at your leaving the house and his being left alone. This is a normal case of separation anxiety, and there are things that can be done to eliminate this problem. Your dog needs to learn that he will be fine on his own for a while and that he will not wither away if he is not attended to every minute of the day. In fact, constant attention can lead to

separation anxiety in the first place. If you are endlessly coddling and cooing over your dog, he will come to expect this from you all of the time and it

DID YOU KNOW?
Dogs left alone for varying lengths of time may often react wildly when you return. Sometimes they run, jump, bite, chew, tear things apart, wet themselves, gobble their food or behave in a very undisciplined manner. Allow them to calm down before greeting them or they will consider your attention as a reward for their antics.

157

Golden puppies want to please you. If you can make your intentions clear to your puppy, he will obey you and be delighted that you are pleased.

DID YOU KNOW?

The number of dogs who suffer from separation anxiety is on the rise as more and more pet owners find themselves at work all day. New attention is being paid to this problem, which is especially hard to diagnose since it is only evident when the dog is alone. Research is currently being done to help educate dog owners about separation anxiety and about how they can help minimise this problem in their dogs.

will be more traumatic for him when you are not there. Obviously, you enjoy spending time with your dog, and he thrives on your love and attention. However, it should not become a dependent relationship where he is heartbroken without you.

One thing you can do to minimise separation anxiety is to make your entrances and exits as low-key as possible. Do not give your dog a long drawn-out goodbye, and do not lavish him with hugs and kisses when you return. This is giving in to the attention that he craves, and it will only make him miss it more when you are away. Another thing you can try is to give your dog a treat when you leave; this will not only keep him occupied and keep his mind off the fact that you just left, but it will also help him associate your leaving with a pleasant experience.

You may have to accustom your dog to being left alone in intervals, much like when you introduced your pup to his crate. Of course, when your dog starts whimpering as you approach the door, your first instinct will be to run to him and comfort him, but do not do it! Really—eventually he will adjust and be just fine if you take it in small steps. His anxiety stems from being placed in an unfamiliar situation; by familiarising him with being alone he will learn that he is okay. That is not to say you should purposely leave your dog home alone, but the dog needs to know that whilst he can depend on you for his care, you do not have to be by his side 24 hours a day.

When the dog is alone in the house, he should be confined to his crate or a designated dog-proof area of the house. This should be the area in which he sleeps and already feels comfortable so he will feel more at ease when he is alone. This is just one of the many examples in which a crate is an invaluable tool for you and your dog, and another reinforcement of why your dog should view his crate as a 'happy' place, a place of his own.

DID YOU KNOW?

There are two drugs specifically designed to treat mental problems in dogs. About 7 million dogs each year are destroyed because owners can no longer tolerate their dogs' behaviour, according to Nicholas Dodman, a specialist in animal behaviour at Tufts University in Massachusetts.

The first drug, Clomicalm, is prescribed for dogs suffering from 'separation anxiety,' which is said to cause them to react when left alone by barking, chewing their owners' belongings, drooling copiously, or defecating or urinating inside the home.

The second drug, Anipryl, is recommended for canine cognitive dysfunction or 'old dog syndrome,' a mental deterioration that comes with age. Such dogs often seem to forget that they were housebroken, where their food bowls are, and they may even fail to recognise their owners.

A tremendous human-animal-bonding relationship is established with all dogs, particularly senior dogs. This precious relationship deteriorates when the dog does not recognise his master. The drug can restore the bond and make senior dogs feel more like their old selves.

COPROPHAGIA

Faeces eating is, to most humans, one of the most disgusting behaviours that their dog could engage in, yet to the dog it is perfectly normal. It is hard for us to understand why a dog would want to eat its own faeces. He could be seeking certain nutrients that are missing from his diet; he could be just plain hungry; or he could be attracted by the pleasing (to a dog) scent. Whilst coprophagia most often refers to the dog eating his own faeces, a dog may eat that of another animal as well if he comes across it. Vets have found that diets with a low digestibility, containing relatively low levels of fibre and high levels of starch, increase coprophagia. Therefore, high-fibre diets may decrease the likelihood of dogs eating faeces. Both the consistency of the stool (how firm it feels in the dog's mouth) and the presence of undigested nutrients increase the likelihood. Dogs often find the stool of cats and horses more palatable than that of other dogs. Once the dog develops diarrhoea from faeces eating, it will likely quit this distasteful habit, since dogs tend to prefer eating harder faeces.

To discourage this behaviour, first make sure that the food you are feeding your dog is nutritionally complete and that he is getting enough food. If changes in his diet do not seem to work, and no medical cause can be found, you will have to modify the behaviour before it becomes a habit through environmental control. There are some tricks you can try, such as adding an unpleasant-tasting substance to the faeces to make them unpalatable or adding something to the dog's food which will make it unpleasant tasting after it passes through the dog. The best way to prevent your dog from eating his stool is to make it unavailable— clean up after he eliminates and remove any stool from the garden. If it is not there, he cannot eat it. Never reprimand the dog for stool eating, as this rarely impresses the dog. Vets recommend distracting the dog whilst he is in the act of stool eating. Another option is to muzzle the dog when he is in the garden to relieve himself; this usually is effective within 30 to 60 days. Coprophagia is seen most frequently in pups 6 to 12 months of age, and usually disappears around the dog's first birthday.

SHOWING YOUR
Golden Retriever

When you purchased your Golden Retriever you will have made it clear to the breeder whether you wanted one just as a loveable companion and pet, or if you hoped to be buying a Golden with show prospects. No reputable breeder will have sold you a young puppy saying that it was definitely of show quality for so much can go wrong during the early weeks and months of a puppy's development. If you plan to show what you will hopefully have acquired is a puppy with 'show potential'.

The first concept that the canine novice learns when watching a dog show is that each breed first competes against members of its own breed.

This is what it's all about. Ribbons, medals and trophies bedeck the walls of famous dog homes. Winning in the show ring indicates that a breeder has been successful in his programme.

DID YOU KNOW?

The Kennel Club divides its dogs into seven Groups: Gundogs, Utility, Working, Toy, Terrier, Hounds and Pastoral.*

*The Pastoral Group, established in 1999, includes those sheepdog breeds previously categorised in the Working Group.

Once the judge has selected the best member of each breed, then that chosen dog will compete with other dogs in its group. Finally the best of each group will compete for Best in Show and Reserve Best in Show.

The second concept that you must understand is that the dogs are not actually competing with one another. The judge compares each dog against the breed standard, which is a written description of the ideal specimen of the breed. This imaginary dog never walked into a show ring, has never been bred and, to the woe of dog breeders around the globe, does not exist. Breeders attempt to get as close to this ideal as possible, with every litter, but theoretically the 'perfect' dog is so elusive that it is impossible. (And if the 'perfect' dog were born, breeders and judges would never agree that it was indeed 'perfect.')

also working trials, obedience trials, agility trials and field trials. The Kennel Club furnishes the rules and regulations for all these events plus general dog registration and other basic requirements of dog ownership. Its annual show

Competing in an all-breed show with your Golden Retriever is an exciting prospect. It takes many years of experience to become a competent, consistent dog handler.

If you are interested in exploring dog shows, your best bet is to join your local breed club. These clubs host shows (often matches and open shows for beginners), send out newsletters, offer training days and provide an outlet to meet members who are often friendly and generous with their advice and contacts. To locate the nearest breed club for you, contact The Kennel Club, the ruling body for the British dog world. The Kennel Club governs not only conformation shows but

called the Crufts Dogs Show, held in Birmingham, is the largest bench show in England. Every year no fewer than 20,000 of the U.K.'s best dogs qualify to participate in this marvellous show which lasts four days. Goldens number among the most popular of show dogs, with thousands competing at Crufts and other major international dog shows each year.

The Kennel Club governs many different kinds of shows in Great Britain, Australia, South

WINNING THE TICKET

Earning a championship at Kennel Club shows is the most difficult in the world. Compared to the United States and Canada where it is relatively not 'challenging,' collecting three green tickets not only requires much time and effort, it can be very expensive! Challenge Certificates, as the tickets are properly known, are the building blocks of champions—good breeding, good handling, good training and good luck!

Show Champion or a Champion. A dog must earn three Challenge Certificates under three different judges to earn the prefix of 'Sh Ch.' or 'Ch.' The Golden Retriever must also prove himself in the field by winning a Certificate of Merit (CM) or earning a Qualifying Certificate (QC). He may earn his QC only after taking his first Challenge Certificate and not before. He is allowed three attempts, and no more than two during one shooting season. Qualifying Certificates may

The Kennel Club encourages Junior Handlers to become involved in dog shows. There is no better education for the next generation of dog people.

Africa and beyond. At the most competitive and prestigious of these shows, the Championship Shows, a dog can earn Challenge Certificates, and thereby become a

be earned at a field trial where at least two 'A' judges are officiating, or at a trial especially designed for dogs who have won their first Challenge Certificates.

Golden Retrievers are popular show dogs around the world. This Golden is an accomplished champion on the Continent.

Challenge Certificates are awarded to a very small percentage of the dogs competing. The number of Challenge Certificates awarded in any one year is based upon the total number of dogs in each breed entered for competition. There two types of Championship Shows, a general show, where all breeds recognised by The Kennel Club can enter, and a breed show, which is limited to a single breed. The Kennel Club determines which breeds at which Championship Shows will have the opportunity to earn Challenge Certificates (or tickets). Serious exhibitors often will opt not to participate if the tickets are withheld at a particular show. This policy makes earning championships ever more difficult to accomplish.

Open Shows are generally less competitive and are frequently used as 'practice shows' for young dogs. There are hundreds of Open Shows each year that can be

DID YOU KNOW?

Just like with anything else, there is a certain etiquette to the show ring that can only be learned through experience. Showing your dog can be quite intimidating to you as a novice when it seems as if everyone else knows what he's doing. You can familiarise yourself with ring procedure beforehand by taking a class to prepare you and your dog for conformation showing or by talking with an experienced handler. When you are in the ring, listen and pay attention to the judge and follow his/her directions. Remember, even the most skilled handlers had to start somewhere. Keep it up and you too will become a proficient handler before too long!

165

Showing is hard work, for the dogs too!

HOW TO ENTER A DOG SHOW

1. Obtain an entry form and show schedule from the Show Secretary.
2. Select the classes that you want to enter and complete the entry form.
3. Transfer your dog into your name at The Kennel Club. (Be sure that this matter is handled before entering.)
4. Find out how far in advance show entries must be made. Oftentimes it's more than a couple of months.

invitingly social events and are great first show experiences for the novice. Even if you're considering just watching a show to wet your paws, an Open Show is a great choice.

Whilst Championship and Open Shows are most important for the beginner to understand, there are other types of shows in which the interested dog owner can participate. Training clubs sponsor Matches that can be entered on the day of the show for a nominal fee. In these introductory-level exhibitions, two dogs are pulled from a hat and 'matched,' the winner of that match goes on to the next round, and eventually only one dog is left undefeated.

There are many obstacles which must be overcome in agility trials for dogs. These trials are almost always very competitive.

Golden Retrievers participating in the Parade of Tartans are favourites of the Scottish and Irish. This event took place in the State of Colorado, USA.

Exemption Shows are similar in that they are simply fun classes and usually held in conjunction with small agricultural shows. Primary shows can also be entered on the day of the event and dogs entered must not have won anything towards their titles. Sanction shows and Limited shows must be entered well in advance, and there are limitations upon who can enter. Regardless of which type you choose, you and your dog will have a grand time competing and learning your way about the shows.

Before you actually step into the ring, you would be well advised to sit back and observe the judge's ring procedure. If it is your first time in the ring, do not be over-anxious and run to the front of the line. It is much better to stand back and study how the

CLASSES AT DOG SHOWS

There can be as many as 18 classes per sex for your breed. Check the show schedule carefully to make sure that you have entered your dog in the appropriate class. Among the classes offered can be: Beginners; Minor Puppy (ages 6 to 9 months); Puppy (ages 6 to 12 months); Junior (ages 6 to 18 months); Beginners (handler or dog never won first place) as well as the following, each of which is defined in the schedule: Maiden; Novice; Tyro; Debutant; Undergraduate; Graduate; Postgraduate; Minor Limit; Mid Limit; Limit; Open; Veteran; Stud Dog; Brood Bitch; Progeny; Brace and Team.

Golden Retrievers can retrieve small birds and well as large game fowl. This dog has retrieved a pigeon.

exhibitor in front of you is performing. The judge asks each handler to 'stand' the dog, hopefully showing the dog off to his best advantage. The judge will observe the dog from a distance and from different angles, approach the dog, check his teeth, overall structure, alertness and muscle

DID YOU KNOW?

You can get information about dog shows from kennel clubs and breed clubs:

Fédération Cynologique Internationale
14, rue Leopold II, B-6530 Thuin, Belgium
www.fci.be

The Kennel Club
1-5 Clarges St., Piccadilly, London W1Y 8AB, UK
www.the-kennel-club.org.uk

American Kennel Club
5580 Centerview Dr., Raleigh, NC 27606-3390, USA
www.akc.org

Canadian Kennel Club
89 Skyway Ave., Suite 100, Etobicoke, Ontario M9W 6R4 Canada
www.ckc.ca

tone, as well as consider how well the dog 'conforms' to the standard. Most importantly, the judge will have the exhibitor move the dog around the ring in some pattern that he or she should specify (another advantage to not going first, but always listen since some judges change their directions, and the judge is always right!) Finally the judge will give the dog one last look before moving on to the next exhibitor.

If you are not in the top three at your first show, do not be discouraged. Be patient and consistent and you will eventually find yourself in the winning lineup. Remember that the winners were once in your shoes and have devoted many hours and much money to earn the placement. If you find that your dog is losing every time and never getting a nod, it may be time to consider a different dog sport or just enjoy your Golden Retriever as a pet.

WORKING TRIALS

Working trials can be entered by any well-trained dog of any breed, not just Gundogs or Working dogs. Many dogs that earn the Kennel Club Good Citizen Dog award choose to participate in a working trial. There are five stakes at both open and championship levels: Companion Dog (CD), Utility Dog (UD), Working Dog (WD), Tracking

Dog (TD), and Patrol Dog (PD). Like in conformation shows, dogs compete against a standard and if the dog reaches the qualifying mark, it obtains a certificate. Divided into groups, each exercise must be achieved 70 percent in order to qualify. If the dog achieves 80 percent in the open level, it receives a Certificate of Merit (COM), in the championship level, it receives a Qualifying Certificate. At the CD stake, dogs must participate in four groups, Control, Stay, Agility and Search (Retrieve and Nosework). At the next three levels, UD, WD and TD, there are only three groups: Control, Agility and Nosework.

Agility consists of three jumps: a vertical scale up a six-foot wall of planks; a clear jump over a basic three-foot hurdle with a removable top bar; and a long jump across angled planks stretching nine feet.

To earn the UD, WD and TD, dogs must track approximately one-half mile for articles laid from one-half hour to three hours ago. Tracks consist of turns and legs, and fresh ground is used for each participant.

The fifth stake, PD, involves teaching manwork, which is not recommended for every breed.

WORKING TESTS

Working tests are frequently used to prepare dogs for field trials, the purpose of which is to heighten the instincts and natural abilities of gundogs. Live game is not used in working tests; the tests are held during the closed season when gundogs are not working or in training. Test organisers set up conditions to simulate as closely as possible an actual shooting event,

and the dogs retrieve dummies on land as well as over water. Unlike field trials, working tests do not count toward a dog's record at The Kennel Club, though the same judges often oversee working tests. Field trials began in England in 1947 and are only moderately popular amongst dog folk. Working tests have, however, grown in popularity as more retriever owners have become involved with training their own dogs.

Whilst breeders of Working and Gundog breeds concern themselves with the field abilities of their dogs, there is considerably less interest in field trials than dog shows. In order for dogs to become full champions, certain breeds must qualify in the field as well. Upon gaining three CCs in the show ring, the dog is designated a Show Champion (Sh Ch). The title Champion (Ch) requires that the dog gain an award at a field trial,

Goldens act like a bunch of kids having their first swim of the season. Goldens love water and you can take advantage of this natural trait by using them as hunting dogs.

Agility trials have become the rage of the dog world. Jumping through a tyre is one of the events at agility trials.

be a 'special qualifier' at a field trial or pass a 'special show dog qualifier' judged by a field trial judge on a shooting day.

FIELD TRIALS

Field titles are amongst the most difficult to achieve because Goldens must compete against other retriever breeds. To become a Field Champion, a Golden Retriever must take two first places at Open or All-Age stakes, with one of those a Variety Stake for all retriever breeds, or win at the annual Retriever Championship Stake. In Ireland, a dog must also have a win, second place or third place on the bench to become an Irish Field Trial Champion.

Field trials are one- or two-day events, depending on the number of dogs entered; anywhere from 12 to 24 are allowed. Applicants are determined by a ballot about a week before the event. In an Open Stake for advanced dogs, a set of three judges and six dogs work in a line moving across a designated field. As the birds are shot, the judges order each individual dog to retrieve. Dogs who do well are called back for further testing. The judges award four placements as well as Certificates of Merit to dogs that have worked commendably but failed to place. A dog who becomes both a Field Trial Champion and a Show Champion is given the difficult-to-earn distinction of Dual Champion.

AGILITY TRIALS

Agility trials began in the United Kingdom in 1977 and have since spread around the world, especially to the United States, where they enjoy strong popularity. The handler directs his dog over an obstacle course that includes jumps (such as those used in the working trials), as well as tyres, the dog walk, weave poles, pipe tunnels, collapsed tunnels, etc. The Kennel Club requires that dogs not be trained for agility until they are 12 months old. This dog sport intends to be great fun for dog and owner and interested owners should join a training club that has obstacles and experienced agility handlers who can introduce you and your dog to the 'ropes' (and tyres, tunnels and so on). The naturally athletic Golden is a natural at such high-level activity, so it is no surprise that Golden owners have embraced the sport with great enthusiasm.

FÉDÉRATION CYNOLOGIQUE INTERNATIONALE

Established in 1911, the Fédération Cynologique Internationale (FCI) represents the 'world kennel club.' This international body brings uniformity to the breeding, judging and showing of purebred dogs. Although the FCI originally included only four European nations: France, Holland, Austria and Belgium (which remains its headquarters), the organisation today embraces nations on six continents and recognises well over 400 breeds of purebred dog. There are three titles attainable through the FCI: the International Champion,

which is the most prestigious; the International Beauty Champion, which is based on aptitude certificates in different countries; and the International Trial Champion, which is based on achievement in obedience trials in different countries. Quarantine laws in England and Australia prohibit most of their exhibitors from entering FCI shows. The rest of the Continent does participate in these impressive canine spectacles, the largest of which is the World Dog Show, hosted in a different country each year. FCI sponsors both national and international shows. The hosting country determines the judging system and breed standards are always based on the breed's country of origin.

DID YOU KNOW?

On the tracking course, Golden Retrievers earn tracking titles that rival the hound breeds known for their scenting prowess. This has a practical function as well...that famous Golden nose also works in search and rescue operations around the world. During every international disaster, from mudslides to earthquakes to terrorist bomb sites, Goldens join the ranks of rescue personnel to help find victims buried beneath the mud or rubble.

INDEX

Page numbers in **boldface** indicate illustrations.

My Golden Retriever

PUT YOUR PUPPY'S FIRST PICTURE HERE

Dog's Name _____

Date _____ Photographer _____